Facts Don't Care About
Your Feelings

Facts Don't Care About Your Feelings

Ben Shapiro

Creators Publishing
Hermosa Beach, CA

FACTS DON'T CARE ABOUT YOUR FEELINGS
Copyright © 2019 CREATORS PUBLISHING

Cover art by Peter Kaminski

CREATORS PUBLISHING
737 3rd St
Hermosa Beach, CA 90254
310-337-7003

ISBN (print): 978-1-949673-16-6
ISBN (ebook): 978-1-949673-15-9

First Edition
Printed in the United States of America
1 3 5 7 9 10 8 6 4 2

A Note From the Publisher

Since 1987, Creators has syndicated many of your favorite columns to newspapers. In this digital age, wc are bringing collections of those columns to your fingertips. This will allow you to read and reread your favorite columnists, with your own personal digital archive of their work.

"Facts Don't Care About Your Feelings" is a collection of columns written by Ben Shapiro. Published between 2016 and 2019, these columns highlight Donald Trump's campaign, election and presidency. The book is divided into 10 chapters that run the gamut from religion to government to the First Amendment and other compelling issues readers on either side of the political aisle will enjoy.

—Creators Publishing

Contents

Flashback

If history repeats itself, and the unexpected always happens, how incapable must Man be of learning from experience.
—George Bernard Shaw

The Group That Got Ignored in Charlottesville

August 16, 2017

The "alt-right" is evil. White supremacism is evil. Neo-Nazism is evil.

I've been saying these things my entire career; I've spent more than a year slamming various factions on the right that refuse to disassociate from and condemn popularizers of the racist alt-right. The media, too, have spent inordinate time covering the rise of the alt-right and tacit acquiescence to it from White House chief strategist Steve Bannon and President Trump. So when an alt-right piece of human debris drove a car at 40 mph into a crowd of protesters in Charlottesville, Virginia, last Saturday, injuring 19 people and killing a 32-year-old woman, the level of scrutiny on the alt-right forced Trump to condemn various alt-right groups by name.

Good.

But the media have remained largely silent about another group: Antifa. Antifa is a loosely connected band of anti-capitalist protesters generally on the far left who dub themselves "anti-fascist" after their compatriots in Europe. They've been around in the United States since the 1990s, protesting globalization and burning trash cans at World Trade Organization meetings. But they've kicked into high gear over the past two years: They engaged in vandalism in violence, forcing the cancelation of a speech by alt-right popularizer Milo Yiannopoulos at the University of California, Berkeley; a few months later, they attacked alt-right demonstrators in Berkeley; they attacked alt-right demonstrators in Sacramento, California, leading to a bloody street fight; they threw projectiles at police during President Trump's inauguration; they attacked pro-Trump free-speech demonstrators in Seattle last weekend. They *always* label their opponents "fascists" in order to justify their violence.

In Charlottesville, Antifa engaged in street violence with the alt-right racists. As in Weimar, Germany, fascists flying the swastika engaged in hand-to-hand combat with Antifa members flying the communist red. And yet, the media declared that any negative coverage granted to Antifa would detract from the obvious evils of the alt-right. Sheryl Gay Stolberg of The New York Times tweeted in the midst of the violence, "The hard left seemed as hate-filled as alt-right. I saw club-wielding 'antifa' beating white nationalists being led out of the park." After receiving blowback from the left, Stolberg then corrected herself. She said: "Rethinking this. Should have said violent, not hate-filled. They were standing up to hate."

Or perhaps Antifa is a hateful group itself. But that wouldn't fit the convenient narrative Antifa promotes and the media buy: that the sole threat to the republic comes from the racist right. Perhaps that's why the media ignored the events in Sacramento and Berkeley and Seattle—to point out the evils of Antifa might detract from the evils of the alt-right.

That sort of biased coverage only engenders more militancy from the alt-right, which feels it must demonstrate openly and repeatedly to "stand up to Antifa." Which, of course, prompts Antifa to violence.

Here's the moral solution, as always: Condemn violence and evil wherever it occurs. The racist philosophy of the alt-right is evil. The violence of the alt-right is evil. The communist philosophy of Antifa is evil. So is the violence of Antifa. If we are to survive as a republic, we must call out Nazis but not punch them; we must stop providing cover to anarchists and communists who seek to hide behind self-proclaimed righteousness to participate in violence. Otherwise, we won't be an honest or a free society.

What Hurricane Harvey Teaches Us About Humanity

August 30, 2017

The pictures, videos and social media posts coming out of Houston, Texas, thanks to Hurricane Harvey are horrifying: children camped out on kitchen counters in order to avoid flooding; elderly women stuck in rest homes and up to their waist in water; tweets from local police departments reminding residents to bring axes into their attic in case they have to cut their way through their roof to escape rising waters. But just as many pictures and videos are inspirational: local men and women hopping into their boats and looking for victims to rescue; police carrying children out of flooded houses; Americans helping one another.

Whenever disaster strikes, we're always inspired by images of human beings helping one another. Disaster often brings out the best in us: our capacity for care, our bravery in risking our lives to help others. Then we're inevitably disappointed in our unending ability to leave those qualities behind the moment disaster ends. We'll rush into burning buildings to save each other, but we'll club each other on the head at political rallies.

Why?

Because there are certain enemies we hold in common. We hold death in common; we'll help all but our worst enemies escape the grave. We hold natural disasters in common as an enemy; we'll react to them by helping out our neighbors. And we hold civilizational threats in common; we'll fight together against the Nazi scourge or the Soviet threat.

But what about when there is no civilizational threat? What about when we're so powerful that serious threats seem unserious? Former President Obama informed us routinely that radical Islamic terrorism didn't threaten our civilization. It's no wonder, then, that so few Americans see radical Islam as a threat worth unifying against. President Trump tells us that Russia isn't a civilizational threat, and neither is global warming. Without a credible existential threat, Americans don't unify.

But there is a credible existential threat to Americans. The problem is that it's internal.

America was built on the foundation of free speech, liberty in personal action, and freedom from violence and governmental tyranny. Those principles are now under attack by groups like antifa, far-left-leaning militants, which maintains that there *is* an existential threat that justifies wartime measures: the presence of the American system itself. Antifa members believe America is steeped in racism, bigotry, economic injustice and police barbarity. And they believe that this gives them the right to carve away at the foundations that hold us together.

This makes them an existential threat, a cancer gnawing at the vitals of the nation. They aren't the only ones, of course: Some violent members of the "alt-right," for example, believe that non-white Americans are the existential threat and use the same logic as antifa. But the true threat to America comes not from outside but from within. It's far harder to unify against that threat if we're unwilling to identify it.

But we should be willing to unify. We should all be willing to defend our neighbors in the peaceful expression of their rights—we should stand with them against violence. We should commit acts of kindness and heroism to help them. There is a storm coming. We must fight it together, or it will overwhelm us while we close our eyes to its danger.

The Power of Good

October 4, 2017

This week, an evil human being murdered nearly 60 Americans and wounded more than 500 others in Las Vegas. His attack was well-planned: The shooter had some 23 guns in his hotel room, including a semi-automatic rifle affixed with a "bump stock" allowing the shooter to operate the rifle like an automatic weapon; he had another 19 guns in his home. Video of the incident is chilling: the rat-a-tat of the gun raining bullets down on unsuspecting innocents from the hulking profile of the Mandalay Bay on the horizon, the wounded concertgoers screaming in the darkness.

But there was heroism, too.

The stranger who threw his body atop Amy McAslin and Krystal Goddard to shield them from the rifle fire. "Just truly incredible," McAslin later said, "a stranger, jumping over me to protect me."

The off-duty nurse from Orange County who told local news that she ran back into the danger to help the wounded: "I'm a nurse and I just felt that I had to ... There was so many people, just normal citizens, doctors, cops, paramedics, nurses, just off duty. ... It was completely horrible, but it was absolutely amazing to see all those people come together."

The anonymous man who threw 18-year-old Addison Short over his shoulder and carried her to safety. The couple who pulled their truck over to carry the wounded to the hospital. The off-duty police using their own bodies to cover the vulnerable. The father who protected his children from gunfire, saying, "They're 20. I'm 53. I lived a good life." Jonathan Smith, a 30-year-old who reportedly saved up to 30 lives, taking a bullet to the neck in the process.

It took hundreds of heroes to save hundreds of people; it took one evil man to wound and kill that many.

On the one hand, it is impossible not to lament the extent of evil: A man attacking those who harmed him in no way, possibly gleefully murdering people attending a concert, makes us wonder at the rot that can infect the human heart. But on the other hand, in each incident of horror we must remember how much the good outweighed the evil. Were there hundreds of people like Stephen Paddock, thousands would have died; were there only one person attempting to stop the impact of Paddock's evil, thousands would have died.

All of which means that as we mourn the victims in Las Vegas, we must also celebrate the heroes. We should see the incident as proof of just how much light infuses America from its citizens—how many normal people run to help each other when evil strikes, when darkness threatens to divide us. So long as that light continues to unite us, America will emerge ready, as always, to fight that darkness.

What an American Hero Looks Like

November 8, 2017

This week, a discharged Air Force airman with a criminal record of domestic abuse, including cracking the skull of his infant stepson, stepped into a church in rural Texas and murdered 26 people, at least a dozen of them children. Americans broke out into their usual arguments over gun control and whether "thoughts and prayers" are helpful; we argued over politicizing tragedy and legislating away rights.

But each time an evil human being decides to attack innocents, it isn't the Twitter battles that stand between the monsters and children. It's heroes. It's men like Stephen Willeford.

In a vacuum, Willeford would be despised by the media. He's a former NRA instructor—you know, the National Rifle Association, a "domestic terror group" devoted to allowing bloodbaths, according to the left. He probably voted for President Trump. His family has lived in Sutherland Springs for four generations. He's parochial enough to attend church regularly. You know, he's a typical bitter clinger.

But when the gunman opened fire, it was Willeford who ran toward the danger. According to Willeford, his daughter told him someone had opened fire at the church half a block away from his home. Willeford immediately ran to his safe and removed his rifle, precisely the type of firearm so many on the left want to legislate out of existence. "I kept hearing the shots, one after another, very rapid shots," Willeford said later, "just 'Pop! Pop! Pop! Pop!' and I knew every one of those shots represented someone, that it was aimed at someone, that they weren't just random shots."

Willeford ran outside with his gun and loaded the magazine. He didn't even bother to put on shoes. And when he saw the piece of human debris responsible for the massacre, he opened fire. "I know I hit him," said Willeford. "He got into his vehicle, and he fired another couple rounds through his window."

The shooter sped away. Willeford hailed another vehicle, and he and the driver began chasing him. That's correct: Civilians chased a shooter through the streets and called 911 on the way. The shooter ended up crashing his car.

Willeford didn't pretend he wasn't afraid. He explained: "I was scared for me. I was scared for every one of them, and I was scared for my own family that just lived less than a block away. I am no hero. I am not. I think my God, my Lord, protected me and gave me the skills to do what needed to be done."

This humble man *is* an American hero. He's what America looks like: people in small towns; churchgoers who quietly raise families and make their communities better; people who have so much to lose because they've built so much without fanfare or reward; people who go running to help their neighbors when they must; men who run toward danger; men with the training and means necessary to stop bad men.

These people have always stood between good and evil. They always will. It won't be laws. It won't be regulations. Laws and regulations failed. Americans—innocent Americans—were murdered because of those failures. More would have died if not for the heroism of Stephen Willeford. Thank God for him.

How to Deal With Bullies

December 13, 2017

This week, America found a new cause to rally around: Keaton Jones. Keaton is a middle school student who was apparently viciously bullied at school for the crime of having a scar on his head from the removal of a tumor. His mother filmed a video of him crying as he explained that other kids had poured milk over his head and mocked him; through his tears, Jones questioned why kids treat one another this way.

The video was absolutely heartbreaking.

It was particularly painful for me. I skipped two grades. By the time I hit sophomore year of high school, I was half a foot shorter and 40 pounds lighter than the other kids. The other kids had been in classes together for years; I was a newcomer. That meant being physically shoved into trash cans and lockers. On one overnight trip, some of my classmates handcuffed me to a metal-framed bed and then hit me repeatedly on the rear with a belt. I pretended to sleep through it, and rather unconvincingly.

So I know what Keaton went through. Being bullied makes you feel like a bottle about to burst—the frustration eats away at your stomach lining and makes you dread going to school. It makes you miserable; even when you're happy, you're constantly waiting for the next shoe to drop.

Still, I don't think Jones' mom should have taken that video.

I think that for two reasons. First, all the celebrity Jones has achieved here won't help him when the cameras turn off. The bullies will still be there, but they'll be twice as cruel, thanks to their belief that he has made fame and fortune off of them. They'll seek to justify their bad actions with more bad actions.

Second, Jones himself isn't going to be helped by this in the long term. No child should have to be bullied, and if someone ever tries to bully my kids, I'll step in with the full range of possibilities at my disposal. But being bullied can have two possible effects: You learn to stand up and cope, or you learn to identify as a victim. If you can hold your head up high even while you're being bullied, you're likely to live a stronger, happier, fuller life. That doesn't mean you're going to be able to knock out the bully a la Daniel in "The Karate Kid." But it does mean you'll be able to better deal with the vicissitudes life has to offer. Those won't end with middle school.

We worry—rightly—about bullying in schools. But we should also worry about how victims treat their victimhood and how they can turn that victimhood into strength for the long haul. Our society has sympathy for victims of bullying, as it should. But we should recognize that just as a wounded animal must be prepared to re-enter the wild lest it die in wild conditions, children must be prepared to live in wild conditions. Those conditions represent life for most people at most times. We can and should stick up for victims against bullies. But we should also focus on empowering victims to become the future bulwarks against bullying—for themselves and for their children.

2019: The Year of the Wokescolds

January 2, 2019

2018 was a chaotic year. It was a chaotic year for the markets, for domestic and international politics, and for social mores. 2019 promises more of the same, if the end of the prior year was any indicator. And it promises something else: the continued rise of the Wokescolds.

Wokescolds are the new representatives of moral panic. We've seen plenty of moral panic before in the United States, from worries about violent video games, to concern about allegations of sex abuse at day care facilities. But never have we seen a moral panic of the stunning breadth of today's woke moral panic. It's a moral panic that insists we change fundamental characteristics of our society, from biology, to language, to politics, to religion, to romantic relations, to art, to comedy.

We're told that if we fail to rewrite biology to suggest there are more than two sexes, or if we don't use preferred pronouns rather than biological ones, we will inevitably create emotional and mental instability among certain vulnerable groups. We're told that if we fail to silence members of groups who haven't suffered sufficiently in the United States, we will be contributing to the perpetuation of power hierarchies that target minorities. We're told that if we don't force religious people to violate their own standards in order to cater to those engaging in what they consider to be sinful activity, we will be bolstering religious oppression. We're told that the only proper type of sexual relationship is one initiated via contractual levels of affirmative consent, rather than mere affirmative body language or acquiescence. We're told that "Baby, It's Cold Outside" and "The Philadelphia Story" are deeply troubling hallmarks of our sexist past (modern rap, replete with brutal degradation of women, is just fine, in case you were wondering). And we're told that if we consider politically incorrect jokes funny, we're strengthening regressive stereotypes.

If we fail to abide by these new strictures, we will be attacked by the Wokescolds. These "woke" inquisitors have apparently mastered the ever-shifting dynamics of leftist power politics and are willing to scour everyone's online history and interpersonal relationships for signs of heresy. Once such heresy is uncovered, the Wokescolds truly go to work: They demand apologies from the supposed sinners and boycotts of those who refuse to disassociate from them. They discourage decent people from speaking up—better to stay silent so as to avoid the wrath of the Wokescolds.

The Wokescolds deliberately pick marginal cases—cases on which good people may be split. This allows the Wokescolds to consistently narrow the boundaries of safety for those who disagree with them.

The latest victim of the Wokescolds: Louis C.K. Now, C.K. has a reprehensible personal history; by his own admission, he used his position of fame and power to lure up-and-coming female comedians backstage, where he would then ask them to watch him touch himself. C.K. has apologized for that behavior. But now he's back on the road, and he's beginning to make jokes again.

This must not be allowed, particularly when his jokes are about such taboo topics as gender pronouns and the alleged expertise conferred by experiencing tragedy. And so C.K. has been pronounced Unwoke. See, before his #MeToo moment, he was sufficiently politically leftist to avoid the Wokescold wrath—after all, he once called Sarah Palin a "c---." But now, C.K. must pay the price for not being sufficiently woke. Those who watch his comedy must be shamed. And we must suggest that he is no longer Funny.

Now, the difference between being funny and being Funny is that when you're funny, everyone knows it—when you're Funny, as defined by critics, you don't have to be funny. You just have to be woke, like the awfully unfunny Hannah Gadsby. *Real humor* requires only satisfying the Wokescolds. We've all just been misdefining comedy for a few millennia.

If all this sounds dull, obnoxious and frustrating, that's because it is. And while the Wokescolds may win temporary victories, those victories will surely be Pyrrhic: As it turns out, we tend to like our biology, language, politics, religion, romantic relationships, art and comedy. The Wokescolds will certainly lose. But not before they destroy a *lot* of people and fray the social fabric nearly beyond repair.

Baby Killing Is Fine. Yearbook Photos Are the Problem

February 6, 2019

Last week, Virginia Gov. Ralph Northam was hit with a shocking blast from the past: a photo on his medical school yearbook page of a man in blackface and another man in a Ku Klux Klan outfit. Northam quickly apologized for the photo, then said he wasn't in the photo and then admitted he had once worn blackface and dressed up as Michael Jackson for a dance contest. He nearly moonwalked at a press conference before his wife gave him a look that could curdle milk.

For this sin—the sin of an old, disgusting, racially insensitive photo—Northam now finds his political career on the skids. As of this writing, he's hanging on by his fingernails, even as his lieutenant governor struggles with dicey sexual assault allegations.

The same week that Northam found himself in hot water, he endorsed a Virginia bill that would have broadened the ability of women to obtain an abortion up to the point of birth. Virginia Delegate Kathy Tran, a sponsor of the bill, stated in defense of her legislation that women would be able to obtain an abortion during *labor*. Northam then defended the bill, adding that if a baby were born alive during such an abortion—he assumed that the abortion would be due to "severe deformities" or "a fetus that's not viable"—then the baby could be "kept comfortable" while the family and the doctor decide its fate.

Even in the least appalling reading of his comments, Northam clearly endorsed infanticide. The only question is whether he endorsed the murder of fully born children.

Yet these comments did not merit his ouster. In fact, they didn't even merit an argument inside the Democratic Party about the extremism of the pro-choice position. Last month, Democrats in the state of New York cheered wildly for a law that opened the floodgates to third-trimester abortion, with Gov. Andrew Cuomo ordering state sites to be illuminated in pink in celebration of the potential murder of the unborn. The Democratic governor of Rhode Island endorsed a similar bill; Democrats in Vermont attempted to pass an even more extreme bill that would enshrine abortion as a "fundamental right" for the entirety of the pregnancy period.

All of this is apparently less controversial than a three-decades-old photograph showing a medical student in blackface. Endorsing the killing of babies during dilation *today*—not 30 years ago, not 30 weeks ago—is considered less of a faux pas than racially offensive idiocy during the Reagan presidency.

The morality of our nation may be skewed beyond repair. Northam certainly deserves criticism for his yearbook stupidities, and for his even more idiotic response. But if the American people are more consumed with the consequences of insulting costumes from 1984 than the murder of the unborn today, we deserve everything we have coming to us.

Can the Super Bowl Save America?

February 8, 2019

It's been several decades since American politics has been so contentious. According to a Reuters/Ipsos poll taken after President Trump's election, 32 percent of California residents want the state to secede from America. In the middle of the election cycle, Public Policy Polling found that 40 percent of Texans would have wanted the state to leave the country if Hillary Clinton had won—and that included 61 percent of Trump supporters. Nationally, 22 percent of people now want to see their particular state leave the union.

All of this is pervading our private lives. One post-election survey showed that nearly 1 in 3 Democrat women have cut someone out of their lives on social media over Trump's election. A September poll from the Monmouth University Polling Institute found that 70 percent of Americans think the election cycle has made America worse.

But we've been able to get together on some things.

We seemed to put aside political differences during the World Series, for example. That communal event—sitting around our televisions watching the greatest Game 7 in baseball history—seemed to unify us. The same thing happened this week with the Super Bowl. We all got together and watched Tom Brady give a performance for the ages, and for a short moment, we got along.

So, here's the question: Is that moment a chimera?

I've long been an antagonist of the notion that bouncing balls can somehow heal real political divisions. In 2007, I wrote this about the World Cup, saying: "Sports solve no great moral dilemmas. Sports are not politics."

That's still true.

But sports *can* provide a breath. Sometimes that breath is actually counterproductive—you wouldn't want a sporting event in

1944 between the United States and Germany to have delayed the liberation of the Nazi death camps by a week. But in America, that breath is highly necessary.

That's because the left has spent so long politicizing every element of American life that we're going to need some space, either physical or temporal. Americans seem willing to part from their neighbors because they believe their neighbors are in a heightened state of readiness to bother them. Texans think Californians want to control how they raise their children; Californians think Texans want to dirty their air. Federalism normally provides the distance for both sides to leave each other alone. But our common culture has shrunk that distance. Now you can't turn on the TV in Dallas without hearing a Los Angeles point of view.

The Super Bowl provided that distance. Thanks to President Trump's election, the Super Bowl organizers clearly recognized— for once—that they'd be best off eschewing politics rather than enabling Beyonce to dance around in Black Panther gear. Lady Gaga did an apolitical halftime show. The game was great. The politics were relegated to easily debunked commercials.

And we all took a breath.

Hollywood and pop culture would do well to remind themselves that if they don't want to alienate half their audience and exacerbate our differences, they can allow us room to breathe. The Super Bowl did that this year. For that, we should be just a little grateful, even if it didn't solve any true underlying problems. Those will require a bit more time and a bit more space.

3 Lessons From the Jussie Smollett Hoax

February 20, 2019

So, Jussie Smollett was lying.

The "Empire" actor claimed that when he was walking home at 2 a.m. in Chicago, in the midst of the polar vortex, he was accosted by two assailants, both of whom shouted anti-gay and anti-black slurs at him. They then attempted to throw a noose around his neck and pour what he thought was bleach on him while shouting, "This is MAGA country!" he says.

None of this is true. Police now believe that Smollett paid two of his friends to stage the entire attack.

Why, exactly, would Smollett do it? He is a successful actor on a hit television show. He's been continuously working in Hollywood for years, with roles in the 2017 films "Marshall" and "Alien: Covenant." He's not exactly a textbook victim.

The answer to this question makes for some uncomfortable lessons.

First, alleged victims sometimes have an incentive to lie. For several years, each time an alleged victim tells an unverified and unverifiable story, we are told that we must believe that victim's story. Why? Because why would the victim lie? But this is often untrue. Smollett had an incentive to lie: unending media attention, fawning sycophancy from politicians and the potential for even greater Hollywood stardom. If Smollett had gotten away with his hoax, he'd be the face of gay, black suffering in the United States. Few had heard of Smollett before this story. Suddenly, he found himself on "Good Morning America," telling the world about his own bravery. That's a lucrative career path.

Second, hoaxers can read the tea leaves. There's a reason that the most prominent racial and sexual hoaxes have generally flattered the political sensibilities of the political left. Right-wing hoaxes might catch the attention of right-wing sources, but left-wing sources are far more powerful and plentiful. Imagine if a MAGA-hatted young Republican had accused two young black men of assaulting him while shouting, "F--- Trump!" That story might get play on talk radio and Fox News, but it wouldn't earn one iota of attention from celebrity culture or the mainstream media.

Third, social media makes hoaxes infinitely easier. There are large-scale incentives for jumping on every story before the facts are clear, which is why both Sens. Cory Booker, D-N.J., and Kamala Harris, D-Calif., both running for president, tweeted their support for Smollett ... and then had to backtrack radically, suggesting as the hoax emerged that they had to wait for more facts. Being the first to rip America bears political fruit; waiting for the whole story often earns public castigation for insufficient sensitivity.

All of this means that the hoaxes won't stop anytime soon. The incentives simply aren't aligned for hoaxes to end. Media members are too eager to buy into stories that support their preferred narratives; social media is too eager to engage in pile-ons of epic proportions; hoaxes are obviously eager to make a buck or win some fame. Which means that we should all wait next time we hear a story too good to be true.

But we won't. Nobody knows who the next Jussie Smollett will be. But within a few weeks, we'll surely know.

The Open Borders Agenda Rears Its Ugly Head

April 10, 2019

This week, President Trump fired his homeland security secretary, Kirstjen Nielsen. Nielsen was, according to media and the Democrats, a monster of the highest order. She was allegedly the force behind the caging of children (that practice began under President Barack Obama and actually ended under President Trump); she was supposedly a barbarian focused on keeping innocent brown children out of America.

And Trump dumped her because even she was not cruel enough to please Genghis Trump, the left claimed. Stephen Colbert joked, "Sure, she put kids in cages, but Trump was upset. ... So he just needs someone who can be crueler to children than Kirstjen Nielsen." Jimmy Kimmel made nearly the same joke: "Goodbye, Kirstjen, and whoever replaces you permanently is going to have some very big cages to fill." Trevor Noah quipped, "Basically, the only job she can get now is working with R. Kelly."

In reality, Trump fired Nielsen because he believed she hadn't properly taken measures to rein in the humanitarian crisis at the border. That was half true—she didn't react with alacrity to change the necessary Homeland Security regulations, for example. But it was also a result of Trump's changing whims with regard to border strategy. Trump was in favor of a no-tolerance border policy that necessarily resulted in family separations; then he was against it; then he was for it; then he was against it.

Most of that vacillation resulted not from brutal bigotry, however, but from a simple fact: Democrats have simply not provided Border Patrol and Immigration and Customs Enforcement with the resources necessary to properly control the border. Federal courts have ruled that families cannot be held together in custody for longer than 20 days; children must be released to guardians outside detention. This means that the Trump administration, like the Obama administration before it, was left with a choice: Either release parents along with children, or separate parents from children.

The federal courts have made the situation even less tenable. They have stated that the Trump administration cannot work with the Mexican government to house potential asylum claimants on the Mexican side of the border to keep families together; they have stated that the Trump administration cannot separate families for prolonged periods of time. A series of conflicting lower-court rulings has left the general policy in limbo.

This means that Congress ought to act. Everyone should be on the same page with regard to those crossing the border illegally. We should have an expedient system for determining the validity of asylum claims; we should give families the option of staying together in detention pending such determination.

But Democrats in Congress refuse to act. They won't change the regulations to allow families to remain together in custody, and they won't provide the funding necessary to keep detained families in some level of comfort. Instead, they snipe at the supposed cruelty of the Trump administration, which simply seeks to end the policy of "catch and release" that results in hundreds of thousands of illegal immigrants remaining indefinitely in the country.

This week, Tom Perez, chairman of the Democratic National Committee, revealed the truth about the Democratic agenda: It's not about compassion at all, but about politics. "Tough doesn't equal smart," Perez stated. "Tough equals dumb." The only truly dumb thing is continuing to play politics with the lives of people crossing the border illegally and American citizens being forced to cope with the price of illegal immigration.

Trump in Office

I need loyalty, I expect loyalty.
—Donald Trump

How Presidents Shape Their Administrations

February 15, 2017

President Trump, we're told by his greatest advocates, will bring much-needed change. Why not merely ignore his rhetorical failings, his unsurpassed egotism, his confident ignorance? There's a good deal that's tempting about this proposal—who wouldn't want to separate the wheat from the chaff? I'm personally on board with perhaps three-quarters of Trump's policy implementation thus far in his presidency, even though I'm deeply concerned by his personal shortcomings. So why not just excise the shortcomings from the roll call?

There's one simple reason: Bureaucrats work toward their bosses. That's as true in the case of authoritarians as it is of democratically elected presidents. Those who live lower on the food chain of the executive branch know that their career advancement is dependent on pleasing the boss. This makes forecasting his desires key to self-preservation.

During President Obama's administration, his underlings attempted to do his bidding without waiting for explicit orders. That's why the IRS targeted conservative charities based on his general statements about Citizens United—they knew what Obama wanted, and they attempted to fulfill his wishes without a smoking gun order.

And indeed, that's what we see from those surrounding President Trump. Rather than hemming him in, they play to him, knowing that if they don't, they're likely to find themselves the recipients of an "Apprentice"-style firing.

Trump is absolutely conspicuous in encouraging such tactics. This week, for example, his senior adviser Kellyanne Conway appeared on national television to slam Nordstrom for its decision to drop Ivanka Trump's fashion line. Conway stated on "Fox &

Friends": "Go buy Ivanka's stuff, is what I would tell you. I hate shopping, but I'm going to go get some for myself today. ... I'm going to give it a free commercial here. Go buy it today." After allegations that this violated federal law, the administration released a statement explaining that Conway had been "counseled." Trump then signaled that he was overweeningly happy with Conway.

The following Sunday, Trump's senior policy advisor, Stephen Miller, made the rounds on the news shows that Trump so conspicuously watches. There, he assured the audience in fully Trumpian language that Trump's power would brook no dissent. Glaring into camera with the confidence of Admiral Motti in "Star Wars" bragging about the Death Star, Miller explained, "I think to say that we're in control would be a substantial understatement." He then added, "our opponents, the media and the whole world will soon see as we begin to take further actions, that the powers of the president to protect our country are very substantial and will not be questioned." He bragged that we will once again have "unquestioned military strength beyond anything anybody can imagine." He said Trump has "accomplished more in just a few weeks than many presidents accomplish in an entire administration." This rather purple language made Trump feel just swell—he tweeted out his congratulations to Miller personally.

Then there was Sean Spicer, Trump's unlucky press secretary, who caved to Trump's ego in the first week and ripped into the media for supposedly underestimating the inauguration crowd size—a particularly sore spot for Trump, obviously. Spicer's awkwardly overheated appearance led Melissa McCarthy to target him on "Saturday Night Live," to the reported discomfort of the president.

All of this is to say that Trump's personality will shape this administration. And that's not a good thing for policy, since he values loyalty over policy and enthusiastic sycophancy over competence. We can only hope that we get some good policy out of Trump before his insecurities overwhelm his administration. Or we can pray that he finally lets those insecurities go and focuses on governing for the benefit of Americans, rather than assuaging his ego and encouraging others to do the same.

What If There's No Plan?

February 22, 2017

"Nobody panics when things go according to plan, even if the plan is horrifying!" the Joker says in "The Dark Knight." "Introduce a little anarchy. Upset the established order, and everything becomes chaos."

Welcome to the Trump administration.

The media seem befuddled as to how the Trump administration handles its business. Upset with the idea that Donald Trump is president, the press have sought a shadow "master planner" in the White House, and they've settled on White House chief strategist Steve Bannon. During the campaign, they suggested that the great mind was then-Trump campaign manager Kellyanne Conway. Sometimes, they say, it's White House senior policy advisor Stephen Miller.

Meanwhile, they see every Trumpian tweet and utterance as 4-D chess. When Trump tweets that the media are the enemy, the media immediately assume Trump has some sort of nefarious plan to quash the First Amendment. When a shoddy report breaks saying that Trump may make federal forces available to work alongside states in cracking down on illegal immigration, they rush to the notion that Trump has formed a deportation squad. When Trump's team rolls out a horribly flawed executive order on immigration from Muslim-majority countries, they immediately conclude that Trump is implementing a Muslim ban.

And what of Trump's bizarre, nonsensical tweets, the ones that don't introduce a new policy? Those are distractions, masterful attempts to hold a shiny object before the public while he plans evil deeds behind the curtain.

Then there are personnel issues. When Trump fires his national security advisor, Michael Flynn, the theories fly fast and furious.

Flynn's connections to Russian President Vladimir Putin will expose Trump, so Trump had to throw him under the bus! Trump *had* to know something, didn't he?

Here's another theory: What if chaos is just chaos?

What if there's no master plan?

What if Trump is finding his way, one step at a time, along a path that 44 other men have traveled, some more slowly than others? What if Trump isn't an ideologue or a philosopher—and what if nobody around him is either? What if it's all just haphazard and chaotic, and what if we don't yet know what this administration will look like?

Is it possible that Trump is simply doing some good things and some bad things, and that he's saying silly things because that's what he does? Is it at all plausible that Trump is the president, not Steve Bannon or Kellyanne Conway or chief of staff Reince Priebus or anybody else, and that because Trump's an amateur at government he's unsure which way to step? Could it be that Trump isn't playing 4-D chess, that he's just a Wookie threatening to upend the board and rip his opponents' arms out of their sockets? He has been known to do that.

All of this is to say, let's all take a deep breath.

Here's the thing: Trump may not have a plan. He probably doesn't. Those around him probably have their own plans, but they're not the president. But you know who *did* have a plan? The people who constructed our constitutional system, placed checks and balances in that system and ensured that no one person could wield all power in American government. That means that even the presidency that begins most chaotically can find its sea legs, and even the presidencies that remain chaotic can't do too much damage.

So let's not panic. Everything's not chaos, even if it feels like it.

The 5 Stages of a Trump Scandal

March 8, 2017

Another week, another "nothing burger" Trump scandal.

This week, President Trump took to Twitter to accuse former President Obama of ordering him to be wiretapped at Trump Tower. That accusation, of course, had no evidence to support it. But instead of merely stating that the accusation was false, the media responded with volcanic rage, declaring that it was *outrageous* to suggest that Obama would *ever* have done such a thing. To this, conservatives rightly responded saying that Obama has a long history of targeting enemies through bureaucratic surrogates, and that multiple media reports stated that the Obama Department of Justice sought FISA warrants against Trump associates. To this, leftists responded by accusing conservatives of covering for Trump's lies.

And so it goes.

This is the typical Trump scandal. It has five stages:

Stage one: A media outlet of Trump's liking reports something.

Stage two: Trump simplifies that report into an incorrect headline.

Stage three: The media jump on the incorrect headline, tacitly suggesting that there is *no* relationship between Trump's headline and the truth.

Stage four: The right fires by pointing out that while Trump may be getting the headline wrong, there's underlying truth to the narrative.

Stage five: The left seethes that anyone would defend Trump's falsehoods.

And then we repeat this routine over and over, further ensconcing ourselves in our partisan bubbles.

We saw this exact pattern just two weeks ago, when Trump saw a piece on Fox News' "Tucker Carlson Tonight" during which video journalist Ami Horowitz traveled to Sweden and talked about rising crime rates related to increased Muslim immigration. Trump took that in, processed it and then blurted out that something awful had happened "last night in Sweden." The media quickly declared that not only had nothing bad happened in Sweden the prior night but that there was also *no* evidence of a serious crime problem in Sweden due to Muslim immigration. To this, the right responded with statistics showing that Sweden did indeed have a rising crime problem, and that lack of statistics did not denote lack of crime but rather politically driven lack of reporting. The media then asked incredulously whether the right would continue to defend Trump's nonsense.

Now, note that nothing here is actually scandalous. Trump will always play fast and loose with the truth; the media will always split hairs in order to declare Trump's entire program out of bounds; and the right will generally defend Trump's larger program. But it does point out a lack of truth telling on all sides because at any stage of this process, the scandal could die. Trump could simply speak accurately. The left could point out Trump's inaccuracies while telling the whole story. The right could do the same.

But because Trump has become such a controversial litmus test, everyone's reacting to Trump rather than to the truth. That means truth becomes secondary, which actually *helps* Trump, since his commitment to the truth is less than strict.

It's time to get beyond this cycle of stupidity. Next time Trump tweets something silly, everybody ought to simply take a deep breath—both left and right. Instead of letting Trump's Twitter feed choose the battleground over facts, Americans on both sides ought to decipher facts and then fight over narrative. That's what decent politics would look like.

When Does Trump Become the Establishment?

March 29, 2017

Let's pretend.

It's January 2017, and President Jeb Bush just took office.

After conceding to his right flank during the election cycle that he would move to overturn President Obama's Deferred Action for Childhood Arrivals program, Bush immediately backtracks and does nothing. Attempting to fulfill a campaign promise, he then pushes a bill that would supposedly repeal and replace Obamacare, except that the bill does no such thing. Instead, it makes significant changes to Medicaid but re-enshrines the central provisions of Obamacare while also creating a new entitlement program. The bill earns the support of establishment stalwarts ranging from House Speaker Paul Ryan, R-Wis., to Senate Majority Leader Mitch McConnell, R-Ky.

Conservatives revolt. They tell Bush that they won't stand by for Obamacare 2.0—they promised repeal and replace, and they'll fulfill their promise. And Bush responds by issuing an ultimatum: It's either this bill or nothing. He'll let Obamacare stand.

Who thinks talk radio would be split? Who believes that Fox News' top hosts would spend the evening stumping for the bill? Who thinks that Bush would be blamed rather than Ryan or McConnell?

If the House Freedom Caucus had defeated the bill, who thinks that many of the anti-establishment conservatives would have mourned?

And if Bush and his top surrogates had then spent the weekend talking about dumping the Freedom Caucus to work with Democrats, who thinks conservatives would have resignedly nodded along?

Of course they wouldn't have. They would have rightly labeled Bush an avatar of the establishment. They would have criticized him for selling out his base, abandoning his supporters and playing to the cocktail party circuit. They would have ripped him up.

But Bush isn't president. Donald Trump is. And because Trump played an anti-establishment figure on TV, too many conservatives assume he is one.

He isn't. President Trump is anti-establishment when it comes to persona, of course—he thinks that every governmental Gordian knot can be cut, that he can simply bulldoze his opposition, that deals are for sissies and that tough guys finish first. But the deals he wants to cut look a lot more like former President George W. Bush's compassionate conservatism than they do like the tea party agenda.

And yet, many Americans keep treating Trump like an outsider. He isn't. He's the most powerful man on Earth, the head of the executive branch. He can't just keep yelling at Ryan and McConnell publicly while dealing with them on legislation that Jeb Bush would endorse in a heartbeat, and then rip conservatives who disagree. That doesn't make him anti-establishment. It just makes him a blowhard.

If Trump wants to represent the outsider, it's about time for him to represent those *outside of government*. And that means minimizing government power, not maximizing it. But that's the dirty little secret: Trump isn't anti-establishment; he's pro-establishment so long as he's the establishment.

Are We Really Living in Trump's America?

April 26, 2017

For the past few months, whenever someone on the left says something particularly insane, conservatives immediately snark back, "This is why Trump won." To a certain extent, they're right: The palpable anger on the radicalized left that helped govern America into political polarization drove the Trump movement. Trump sits in the White House as a result.

But there's a more important question that must be asked as we approach day 100 of the Trump administration: Has Trump actually changed anything in America?

The 100-day mark means little in reality. As Trump points out, it's an arbitrary deadline; there have been presidents who did little in their first 100 days and ended up with a solid legacy (Bill Clinton) and those who did an enormous amount and ended up imploding (Lyndon B. Johnson). But here's what the first 100 days *actually* do: They set the table.

President Ronald Reagan set the table for his administration by pushing for lower taxes over the protestations of the Democrats and militantly standing against Soviet aggression. President Clinton's failures in his first 100 days set the stage for his move to the center—by his second term, he declared that the "era of big government is over."

President Barack Obama came into office promising change. That change did not come chiefly in the realm of policy—his only lasting policy change appears to be Obamacare, which is currently bankrupting itself across the country—but in the political heart of the country. Before 2009, Americans yearned for unity. It's why Obama was elected. We were tired of the polarization of the Bush years; we were sick of the feeling that half the country wanted the other half gone. Obama pledged to change that.

That pledge came on the back of big-government promises. America could be united, Obama seemed to suggest, if only we believed in him personally. *That's* what Obama achieved in his first 100 days: He changed the nature of the political debate by suggesting that big government could earn your trust, that he would demonstrate the dedication necessary to turn government into an avatar of this newfound "unity."

Then he utilized government power to push for hardcore leftism, which polarized the country.

Obama's 100-day vision failed. But Trump has yet to replace it with anything new. Trump's "Make America Great Again" sloganeering hasn't promised a new unity of purpose. It has actually exacerbated a reverse polarization. His policies aren't discussed in terms of helping all Americans; they embody a political sectarianism pioneered by Obama and hijacked by Trump. Trump's first 100 days haven't moved the American story in any marked way at all, actually—we're precisely where we were 101 days ago. That doesn't mean he hasn't had policy victories (most obvious is the confirmation of Supreme Court Justice Neil Gorsuch). But it *does* mean that there is no vision upon which he calls Americans to the table. There are just things he wants and things he doesn't, and Americans he likes and Americans he doesn't.

If past trends hold, that means his administration will continue to be a haphazard agglomeration of random partisan prescriptions without any basis in a thoroughgoing vision of Americanism. We're all here, and he's the president, and that's that. But while such lack of vision can work in an oppositional setting, as a rejection of the status quo, it can't move America forward in any real way.

That's why Trump must decide what he wants America to be, not just what he wants Americans to think of him. He must provide a vision. If he doesn't, he'll be seen as merely a placeholder, a reactionary president living in an America of Barack Obama's making.

Can a Bad Man Be a Good President?

January 29, 2018

This week, FBI deputy director Andrew McCabe—a man who certainly should have stepped down months ago—finally resigned from his active role at the agency. McCabe had been under President Trump's fire for months given his failure to recuse himself from the Hillary Clinton email investigation despite his wife having received nearly $700,000 in campaign donations from Clinton associates during her failed Virginia state senatorial race.

Shortly after his resignation hit the headlines, another story broke from NBC News: The day after Trump fired then-FBI Director James Comey, Trump was astonished and angered to learn that Comey had been offered a flight home on an FBI airplane. He allegedly called up McCabe and reamed him for allowing it. When McCabe dissented from Trump's diatribe, Trump told McCabe that he ought to "ask his wife how it feels to be a loser," apparently referring to her election loss.

This is, to put it mildly, gross.

But Trump isn't exactly shy about his grossness. "Loser" is one of his favorite terms of art. Among other recipients of that accolade are Mark Cuban, George Will, former White House deputy chief of staff Karl Rove, actor Richard Belzer, Scottish farmer Michael Forbes, Glenfiddich scotch whiskey and the GOP as a whole. The list goes on.

All of this has been brushed off by conservatives. After all, Trump is providing some of the most conservative policy of the last half-century. Not only has he signed a massive tax cut into law but he has also slashed regulations, repealed the individual mandate, nominated conservative judges, moved the American embassy in Israel to Jerusalem, supported the anti-Iranian alliance in the Middle East and moved to box in Russia. He has presided over massive economic growth at home and the collapse of the Islamic State group in Syria and Iraq.

Trump's list of accomplishments should seemingly answer a question with which conservatives have been struggling: Can a bad man make a good president? The answer, obviously, should be yes.

What's more, the answer should have been obvious: Machiavelli suggested back in the 16th century that perhaps *only* a bad man can be a good politician. Machiavelli stated that virtue is an unrealistic and counterproductive standard for a statesman—what is needed is *virtu*, a capacity to use virtue and vice for the achievement of a specific end. Even Aristotle, a devotee of virtue, suggested that good citizens need not be good men.

All of which makes sense. Bad men make great artists. Bad men make great athletes. Saints often die in penury; sinners often die in riches.

But Trump's list of accomplishments is only half the story. That's because the office of the presidency is about more than mere accomplishments: It's about modeling particular behavior. Bill Clinton was a successful president, but he was not a good one: He drove the country apart, degraded our political discourse and brought dishonor to the White House. The same was true for President Richard Nixon. Doing good things as president does not mean being a good president. Being a good president requires a certain element of character.

And Trump's character is still lacking. Perhaps in the end, conservatives should ignore Trump's character defects and take the wins; I certainly cheer those wins. Perhaps in the end, Trump's character will poison the wins themselves; we won't know that for years. We do know, however, that if we believe the president has two roles—one as a policymaker, the other as a moral model—then President Trump can only be half-successful so long as he refuses to change himself.

Trump's Triumph or Kim's Coup?

June 13, 2018

This week, President Trump went to Singapore to meet with the most repressive dictator on the planet, North Korean Supreme Leader Kim Jung Un. Kim presides over a slave state of 25 million people, with gulags stacked with hundreds of thousands of political dissidents. He has diligently pursued nuclear weapons and long-range missile tests. He was greeted as a celebrity in Singapore, with President Trump shaking his hand, calling him "very smart" and "a funny guy" and generally praising him to the skies.

Fans of President Trump were ecstatic. To them, this was a breakthrough movement: an American leader sitting down with a North Korean leader, finally breaking through the clutter of the past to get down to brass tacks. To Trump critics, this was a debacle: The president handed Kim an unprecedented propaganda coup, complete with grinning photos and thumbs up before a backdrop of interpolated North Korean and American flags.

Here's the truth: We don't know what this will be yet. If it turns out that Trump has a trick up his sleeve—if it turns out that Trump has indeed convinced Kim to denuclearize and liberalize his country—then this will go down in history as a move of extraordinary genius. If, however, it's a photo op designed to allow Trump to claim status as a diplomatic wizard, and if Kim gives up nothing while the United States legitimizes an evil tyrant and ratchets down military exercises with South Korea, it will be a debacle.

This was a high-risk, high-reward strategy.

But it doesn't appear that the White House thinks of it that way. Instead, it seems to view the summit as an unalloyed win for President Trump no matter what happens next. Trump, they say, can always reverse himself. Trump himself made the same point:

"Honestly, I think he's going to do these things. I may be wrong. ... I don't know that I'll ever admit that, but I'll find some kind of an excuse."

And herein lies the problem. Trump has a stake in *not being wrong*. That's why presidents typically don't hold face-to-face get-togethers with evil dictators until some sort of serious negotiation has already taken place. Trump is now invested in the success of his diplomacy, rather than in the strongest possible outcome alone. That's a win for Kim, at the very least. Trump has given Kim an advance against the possibility of future concessions. If those concessions never materialize, Trump will be forced to choose between admitting he was bamboozled and brazening through the humiliation, pretending that Kim is in fact a moderate force willing to work with him.

Right now, barring additional evidence of North Korean surrender, Kim has the upper hand. That could always change tomorrow; we should hope and pray that it will. If it doesn't, then President Trump not only won't get a win out of the North Korean summit; he'll have been played by a tin-pot dictator with a penchant for murdering his family members.

Is Collusion Criminal?

August 8, 2018

In the last two weeks, the Trump administration has begun to make a rather interesting legal argument: Collusion isn't criminal. President Trump's lawyer Rudy Giuliani made this argument on television; Trump repeated it on Twitter. But is it true?

Technically, collusion isn't a crime. There is no statutory definition of "collusion"; the closest we could come is "conspiracy." So let's be more specific: Would it be criminal activity if the Trump campaign solicited opposition research from the Russian government? The short answer: Not clearly, unless the campaign was also involved in underlying criminal activity, such as hacking the Democratic National Committee or the Hillary Clinton campaign. UCLA professor of law Eugene Volokh explained in the Washington Post last year that barring such activity, it seems violative of the First Amendment to prevent campaigns from talking with foreign citizens about opposition research on other candidates. After all, Clinton's team paid Fusion GPS to create an opposition-research dossier, much of the material provided by a foreign citizen, Christopher Steele. Even exchanging information with the Russian government wouldn't clearly violate the law, if Volokh is correct.

Now, this doesn't mean that the Trump campaign is in the clear. It just means that Trump's opponents will have to prove far more than they've proved so far.

All of which means that the slim hook on which the Democratic hopes of a Trump criminal charge are based grows even more tenuous. Now Democrats are banking on the possibility of an obstruction charge emerging against Trump: perhaps, they say, Trump has attempted to shut down special counsel Robert Mueller's investigation in some way. After all, he's constantly tweeting about the myriad evils of the so-called "witch hunt." But even here, the statutory basis for such a charge is thin: There are provisions covering destruction of evidence or threatening to influence a "pending judicial proceeding," but obstruction generally requires an active attempt to impede—and the Mueller investigation, according to the testimony of Deputy Attorney General Rod Rosenstein, hasn't actually been impacted by Trump's fulmination.

The best hope for Democrats is a perjury charge against Donald Trump Jr. They hope that Trump Jr. lied when he said that his father didn't know about the June 2016 Trump Tower meeting with Russian lawyer Natalia Veselnitskaya; perhaps, they think, they can charge Trump Jr. with something to get him to flip on his father. But so far, there's been no evidence that Trump knew about that meeting, and Trump continues to deny it.

More and more, the Democratic hope for a deus ex machina to oust Trump seems like a chimerical fancy. (Even if Trump were to be indicted for a crime, it's utterly unclear constitutionally whether he could be prosecuted; the constitutional remedy for high crimes and misdemeanors is impeachment.) But they do have one hope yet: Trump could continue to pour out his feelings on Twitter, creating possible legal problems for himself and undermining his credibility with the American people.

That's why Trump should stop chatting about these matters. The more he chats, the higher the chances he creates a thicket he cannot escape. The Democrats' best hope at this point isn't the law or even Robert Mueller. It's President Trump's rage, and his pathological inability to avoid venting it in public fora.

The Myth of Obama, the Myth of Trump and the Reality of Elections

November 7, 2018

In the aftermath of this week's midterm elections, in which Democrats gained 34 House seats and lost an additional three Senate seats, an odd emotional disconnect took place. Democrats, who had just won control of the House, seemed disappointed in their victory; they had expected a sweeping tsunami to carry them from Arizona across Texas and through Florida. They seemed borderline despondent that their extraordinarily dislike for President Trump hadn't translated into historic gains. Meanwhile, Republicans, who had just surrendered the speakership to Nancy Pelosi, were somewhat giddy; they immediately paid homage to President Trump for his stunning work in preventing Democrats from marking up big wins in Florida and Ohio.

All of this seems somewhat misguided.

The disparate reactions of the two political parties are predicated on a foundational myth about modern American politics: the myth of Barack Obama. According to the Obama Myth, once upon a time, America was divided between red and blue on the basis of right-left politics. Then, along came President Obama, who won two sweeping electoral victories, forging a coalition of intersectional identity groups in emergent demographic groups and utterly reshaping the electoral map in a permanent way.

For Democrats, the Obama Myth leads them to see President Trump's 2016 as an electoral aberration—a momentary spasm of the American public, soon to be corrected. Any indicator that 2016 was more of a trend than an outlier cuts against the Obama Myth.

For Republicans, the Obama Myth leads them to believe in the Trump Myth. The Trump Myth suggests that once upon a time, there was a land dominated by an intersectional coalition set to rule in perpetuity. Then along came Donald Trump, who broke apart the blue wall and set in its place a new movement, populist and deep. This myth portrays President Trump as an electoral magician, a man defying gravity and leading Republicans into uncharted new lands of victory. Its adherents become willing to attribute every victory to Trump and every loss to lack of Trump—a theory Trump actively promotes by slamming Republican politicians who fail to embrace him sufficiently.

But here's the thing: The Obama Myth is a myth, and so is the Trump Myth. The reality is that the electoral aberration was not Trump but Obama. Trump isn't a magician; he's a regression to the electoral mean. Here are the percentages of the vote won by Republican presidential candidates in 2000, 2004, and 2016 in Ohio: 50.0, 50.8, 51.3. Here are those numbers for Florida: 48.9, 52.1, 48.6. For Wisconsin: 47.6, 49.3, 47.2. For Pennsylvania: 46.4, 48.5, 48.2. For Michigan: 46.1, 47.8, 47.3.

Trump didn't significantly overperform in any of these states. He did what Republicans, absent Obama, did in 2004 and 2000.

What, then, was 2016? 2016 was an odd combination of a regression to the Republican mean and Hillary Clinton's incredible incompetence, as well as low Democratic turnout thanks to their belief that she would surely win. That's why we shouldn't be surprised by last night's results. Republicans performed as they've always performed outside of Obama. Democrats performed as they've always performed outside Obama.

So, what lesson should Republicans learn? That political gravity applies to President Trump—and that they've got to reach out to the suburban voters they lost in the midterms. What lesson should Democrats learn? The Republican Party remains competitive in swing states, and running to the hard progressive left while shouting about Trump won't cut it.

Will either party learn those lessons? Probably not. So buckle up. It's going to be a wild two years.

The News Cycle Without Trump's Tweets

July 17, 2019

Let's pretend President Trump didn't tweet.

Let's live in a universe where the president of the United States didn't see fit to insert himself into every controversy, to comment on every passing event, to blast out his inner monologue before tens of millions of Americans each morning—often in the most foolish, controversial or outright xenophobic way—while watching cable news.

Here's what the news cycle would look like.

Last week, House Speaker Nancy Pelosi, D-Calif., went to war with the most famous member of her House contingent, freshman Congresswoman Alexandria Ocasio-Cortez, D-N.Y. After months of vacillating between praise for AOC's supposed energy and put-downs of AOC's radicalism and attacks on moderate Democrats, Pelosi's sneering finally triggered AOC, who promptly brought out her heavy guns: She suggested that Pelosi is a racist targeting congresswomen of color. She even suggested that Pelosi is responsible for the death threats she had received. This, in turn, triggered members of the Congressional Black Caucus to come to Pelosi's defense, and that triggered other members of AOC's so-called squad to come to her defense. By the end of the week, the seething, bubbling war between radicals and mere progressives was threatening to crack the Democratic coalition.

Also last week, Democratic presidential candidates continued their quest to push their party toward the far left. Sen. Kamala Harris, D-Calif., maintained her hypocritical attacks on former President Joe Biden for his lack of support for federal busing, a policy she herself doesn't support. Sen. Elizabeth Warren, D-Mass., trotted out a new spending plan with no way to pay for it. Harris and Warren prepared to attack each other for attention. Meanwhile, virtually all the major Democratic candidates outside of Biden kept up their drumbeat of criticism of Immigration and Customs Enforcement, demanding an open-borders agenda entirely at odds with the mainstream of American public thought.

This drumbeat came complete with an actual act of violence, as well as a public relations nightmare for the open-borders left. In Washington state, 69-year-old Willem Van Spronsen, armed with a rifle and incendiary devices, attempted to light a car on fire and ignite a propane tank outside a Tacoma migrant detention center to shut it down. He was shot for his trouble. Van Spronsen reportedly called himself a member of antifa, the far-left militant group.

And in Aurora, Colorado, some 2,000 people banded together outside another ICE detention facility, where a group of protesters pulled down the American flag and replaced it with the Mexican flag. Some of the protesters then attempted to burn and deface the American flag with anti-police slurs.

This would seem to have been a pretty decent news cycle for President Trump. The Democratic Party formed itself into a circular firing squad; the far left was busily reminding Americans that it's not especially fond of America altogether.

Then Trump tweeted.

For years, we've heard that Trump's tweeting is a key to his success. There's certainly truth to the notion that Trump is able to redirect the news cycle toward his personal whims based on the click of a few buttons. But with great power comes great risk. When the president decides to tweet, "'Progressive' Democrat Congresswomen...originally came from countries whose governments are a complete and total catastrophe ... Why don't they go back and help fix the totally broken and crime infested places from which they came," the narrative shifts. The news cycle becomes about Trump's xenophobia (three of the congresswomen he's apparently talking about were born in the United States); Democrats reunite against him; and the dangers of anti-ICE rhetoric are deliberately obscured by the media.

All too often, Trump's tweets are bad, both morally and politically. And the media would always prefer to jabber about those tweets than about news that harms Democrats. So why would Trump continue to provide them the oxygen they so desperately seek?

The Left's Thought Fascism

Nationalizing businesses, nationalizing banks, is not a solution for the democratic party, it's the objective.
—Rush Limbaugh

The Left Can't Help Overplaying its Hand

January 18, 2017

This week, Rep. John Lewis, D-Ga., accused President-elect Donald Trump of being an illegitimate president. He said: "I think the Russians participated in helping this man get elected. And they helped destroy the candidacy of Hillary Clinton. ... When you see something that is not right, not fair, not just, you have a moral obligation to do something."

Lewis wasn't the only person claiming that Trump had been elected illegitimately. New York Times columnist Paul Krugman, who just last week was preaching about why it's important to "(be) a mensch," wrote that it is "an act of patriotism" to "declare the man about to move into the White House illegitimate." Jehmu Greene, a Democratic National Committee chair candidate, said that Trump was "allegedly elected."

In response, another DNC chair candidate, Rep. Keith Ellison, D-Minn., upped the ante. He said he wouldn't be attending the inauguration because "(He) will not celebrate a man who preaches a politics of division and hate." Ellison spent most of his career lauding the hateful and divisive Nation of Islam.

Meanwhile, Trump met with Martin Luther King III at Trump Tower; King emerged in the lobby after the meeting and explained: "(Trump) said that he is going to represent all Americans. ... I believe that's his intent, but I think we also have to consistently engage with pressure, public pressure." Trump also met with entertainer Steve Harvey; they discussed poverty and incoming Housing and Urban Development Secretary Dr. Ben Carson, and Harvey then stated: "I found him in our meeting both congenial and sincere. Trump wants to help with the situations in the inner cities. ... I walked away feeling like I had just talked with a man who genuinely wants to make a difference in this area."

So, do most Americans believe that Trump is a vicious racist, an illegitimate president who must be treated with scorn and disdain? Of course not. While Trump is highly unpopular for an incoming president—he has the lowest approval rating in modern history, at 40 percent—nearly all Americans think Trump was elected legitimately.

A majority of them don't think Trump is racist.
Yet the left continues to double down on fiction instead of banking on fact.

In the past, the media and the Democrats were able to peddle extreme fictions because they had more powerful bullhorns than their targets. Former Gov. Mitt Romney could safely be labeled a tax cheat by Sen. Harry Reid, D-Nev., without fear of being blasted with a public relations tsunami; Vice President Joe Biden could state that Romney wanted to put black people back in chains; President Barack Obama could lie about the state of U.S.-Russia relations; the media could trot out old, unsubstantiated stories about Romney's supposed gay-bashing. And Romney couldn't do a thing.

That's not the case with Trump. Love him or hate him, Trump knows how to get attention, and his 20 million followers on Twitter give him quicker access to a wider audience than virtually any single media outlet or personality. That means the media and the Democrats need to button up their criticism rather than throw the kitchen sink.

But they're used to throwing the kitchen sink.

One problem: Trump has a public relations trebuchet, and he'll simply launch every kitchen appliance available in response.

If the left wants to keep marginalizing itself, it ought to continue leveling every radical allegation it can find against Trump. If the left wants to defeat Trump, it should stick to the facts.

Given recent history, that seems highly unlikely.

The Left Won't Stop Threatening Violence Against Trump

February 1, 2017

We're barely a week and a half into President Trump's administration, and the left is in sheer panic mode. We've seen headlines blaring that Trump instituted a Muslim ban (he didn't). We've seen speculation that the Trump White House's failure to clearly inform the Department of Homeland Security how to implement his immigration executive order amounts to an attempted coup (nope). We've seen accusations that Trump will overthrow the judiciary, run roughshod over Congress and generally make a fascist nuisance of himself.

This isn't good for the country.

That's because if you think Trump is Literally Hitler, you're more likely to endorse violence against him and his allies, which is precisely what leftists have begun doing. At the Screen Actors Guild Awards, "Stranger Things" star David Harbour threatened Trump supporters over his immigration/refugee executive order, saying, "And when we are lost amidst the hypocrisy and the casual violence of certain individuals and institutions, we will, as per Chief Jim Hopper, punch some people in the face when they seek to destroy the meek and the disenfranchised and the marginalized." Madonna spoke at the Women's March on Washington, saying that she has "thought an awful lot about blowing up the White House." Robert De Niro said back in October that he'd like to "punch (Trump) in the face." Actress Lea DeLaria of "Orange Is the New Black" said that she wanted to "pick up a baseball bat and take out every f--king republican and independent I see."

Violence only becomes acceptable in the minds of most people if they are the victims. And not just victims—ultimate victims. They must have no other option. That means that playing up the threat of a

Trumpocalypse means heightening the likelihood of violence. And we have indeed seen isolated incidents of anti-Trump violence around the country, dating all the way back to the campaign, when the media simply ignored Black Lives Matter movement attempts to shut down Trump campaign events.

Once we have reached the point where overt tearing of the social fabric is seen by half the country as morally decent, there is no more social fabric to tear. Civilization is actually on the ropes.

Which means that everybody has an obligation to calm the hell down.

Civilization isn't going to end because many Americans don't like Trump's policies. And Americans still have the ability to resist politically without engaging in violence. The left believes that it has a monopoly on nonofficial violence, which is why former President Barack Obama shied away from the harsh condemnation of riots in major American cities. But all that did was fray the social fabric to the point where tribalism has become mainstream political discourse.

Now we're even a step beyond that. No longer does the left restrict its vision of political violence to the already-immoral claim that downtrodden black folks in failing cities should be given "space to destroy." Upper-class elites at the SAG Awards have permission to engage in violent rhetoric. Everybody is capable of getting violent now that Trump is here.

Which means that political violence will likely increase. Which, counterproductively for the left, means that Trump will use the power at his disposal to restore law and order. And so the cycle will continue.

Why Does It Feel Like Everything's a Scandal?

March 22, 2017

Over the past two weeks, Democrats have begun to acknowledge that they have virtually no evidence demonstrating meaningful collusion between the Trump campaign and the Russian government. They proclaim that circumstantial evidence shows ties between Trump staffers and President Vladimir Putin—former Trump campaign manager Paul Manafort and former Trump advisor Roger Stone allegedly had significant contacts with the Russians. But to this point, they've got nothing.

Meanwhile, the FBI director and head of the National Security Agency announced that they had no evidence that Trump Tower was wiretapped by former President Obama. Mike Rogers, the NSA head, agreed that any accusations of British intelligence involvement in Trump wiretapping is "ridiculous." Republicans point to the fact that there were multiple media reports of Trump associates being caught on wiretap. But to this point, they've got nothing.

Scandals that catch fire require two elements: first, confirmation of a widely held suspicion about a politician's character; second, actual evidence of nefarious behavior. Hillary Clinton's email scandal damaged her significantly because of her long record of untrustworthy behavior, including destruction of records. Bill Clinton's sex scandal damaged him because he had a long history of lying about his sexual conduct.

Other scandals simply never gained steam because they lacked the requisite plausibility, even if the evidence was sufficient. Yes, the IRS should have damaged President Obama. But the central contention that Obama used government as an instrument to target his opposition never took hold of the public imagination. Sure, Iran-Contra should have severely tarnished President Reagan. But Americans didn't buy the notion of Reagan as a great international manipulator. In short, politicians we trust more are less likely to suffer from severe scandal.

And herein lies the problem: In an era in which half of the population will believe virtually everything about the other side, we're primed for scandal *all the time*. The tinder of scandal is dry, and everyone is just waiting nervously for a lit match to set the blaze. That means a whiff of scandal pervades nearly everything. Otherwise-innocuous behavior seems laden with sinful potential. And those who claim wrongdoing about those on the other side gain additional credibility *no matter the evidence of what they claim*.

That means the conspiracy theorists gain ground while honesty loses. Those on the left willing to accuse President Trump of Kremlin connections sans evidence earn the love and support of those on their own side of the aisle; and those on the right willing to humor Trump's most extreme claims about Obama's wiretapping gain clicks and admiration on their side. The result: Those who suggest that we wait for evidence are seen as gullible, naive.

In this context, the space for rational conversation shrinks down to a thimble. Instead of the left dismissing President Trump's stupidities as stupidities, Trump becomes a nefarious character seeking doom; instead of the right acknowledging that intelligence could have swept up some Trump contacts in its pursuit of Russian interference, the entire intelligence community becomes a big blob of statist corruption. No mistake is honest; every action must be interpreted in the darkest possible way.

If this leads to an American return to smaller government—hey, we can't trust anybody anyway, so let's stop handing them power—this new paranoia might be acceptable. But it won't. Instead, Americans seems bound and determined to hand power to those on each side who are most apt to identify the nefarious intentions of those on the other side, with or without evidence. That's a recipe for not only polarization but also political breakdown.

The Democrats Lose Their S---

April 19, 2017

Donald Trump won the presidency because he was seen as blunt and non-manipulative, as opposed to the robotic, incompetent Machiavellianism of Hillary Clinton—and because he demonstrated that he cared about the concerns of Americans who were sick of being called racist sexist bigot homophobes for not paying obeisance to the leftist cause du jour.

Democrats apparently think he won because he said the word "s---."

On Wednesday, the Democratic Party got into a Twitter war with the Republican Party. The GOP tweeted out a picture of a shirt sold by the Dem rats that says "Democrats give a sh*t about people." This is a takeoff on Democratic National Committee Chairman Tom Perez's statements that Republicans don't give a s--- about people. Republicans responded to the shirt by tweeting: "2016: 'When they go low, we go high'—Michelle Obama." The Democratic Party responded, "Taking away health care from 24 million people is going low. Giving a s--- about people is going high."

The theory here seems to be that repeating the same Democratic message but with a higher pitch and more vulgar language will win them political favor again. It wasn't Trump's rejection of leftism that won him acolytes; it was that he dropped the S-word and the F-word and the P-word. If only Democrats could imitate his style—all would be well!

This is asinine.

Cursing didn't hurt Trump because Trump was running *against* type. His cursing demonstrated that he wasn't a conservative fuddy-duddy who was deeply concerned about policing language. He channeled the anger of his base.

Democratic cursing just demonstrates, as always, that Democrats have no standards with regard to speech. It's not violating a taboo to say s--- as a Democrat because there is no taboo. And simply saying that word over and over doesn't help Democrats who are still struggling for a national message.

Democrats are in trouble nationwide because they have strayed from their core pitch: caring about every American. Instead, they have decided to embrace the intersectional nonsense of Barack Obama, who divvied Americans up along race, class, sex and sexual orientation lines and then pandered to each group individually. That program is both anti-American and insincere because to pander to each group means to shortchange them all. After all, what happens when Democrats claim that black Americans are victims of white society but that gay Americans are victims of straight society? Are black straight people the victims or the victimizers? Is the unemployed blue-collar white fellow who used to work a steel job in Indiana the victim because he's living on the edge of poverty, or is he the victimizer because he refuses to agree that a biological man can be a woman?

The Democrats no longer have a national message that resonates. They have regional messages that make most Americans feel like refuse. But because Democrats think that they'll only win by upping their "cool factor," they'll continue trotting out Sarah Silverman to make vagina jokes in a little girl voice while mocking Donald Trump and then believe they've won the cultural battle. They'll deploy Tom Perez to use other four-letter words.

And they'll keep losing.

Racism Is Only Racism If Comes From Groups the Left Hates

May 10, 2017

This week, an odd tweet appeared in my mentions from verified Twitter users—users prominent enough to be granted a blue check mark by Twitter itself. This one came courtesy of a rapper named Talib Kweli Greene. I'll admit I'd never heard of Greene until he suddenly appeared in my mentions calling me a "racist ass." It turns out Greene is a rapper with well over 1 million Twitter followers and a long history of "social activism."

A quick search of Greene's Twitter feed showed a wide variety of instances of the rapper calling people "white boy" and "coon." He says that this does not make him racist, of course—only the term "black boy" would be racist, since Greene maintains that white people cannot truly be victimized by racism. When I pointed out that seeming incongruity, Greene replied: "What's the problem white boy? You think 'white boy' is racist? Wow. You're dumber than I thought." He then dared me to call him "black boy," which, of course, I would never do, since that would be racist.

What's Greene's actual argument? It seems to be that since the derogatory slur "black boy" was thrown around by lynch mobs, any other derogatory slur can no longer be derogatory. This is the rhetorical equivalent of the argument your mother used to make back in grade school: You're not truly hungry, since there are children in China who are starving to death. The argument fails for the same reason: Yes, it turns out there are gradations of racism, just as there are gradations of hunger. But you *were* hungry when you were a kid, even if your bowels weren't distended, and you're a racist if you call someone "white boy" in a derogatory fashion, even if you're not attempting to lynch him.

Thanks to the theory of intersectionality, however, such logic goes by the wayside. Intersectional theory has now taken over the college campuses, leaving the broken corpses of decency and reason in its wake. Intersectionality classifies social categories of race, class, gender and sexual orientation into a hierarchy of victimhood that decides how you should be treated. If you are a black lesbian, for example, you outrank a black straight man and your view must be treated with more care and weight than that of the black straight man. More importantly, since society somehow classifies you as "lesser" than the black straight man, you are incapable of ever doing anything to victimize that black straight man—social powerlessness means that your individual victim status never changes.

This is why Greene and others on the left believe it's just fine to use "white boy" as a slur: Black people have historically seen discrimination in America that whites have not; whites benefit from a more powerful status in society at large; and therefore, black people cannot possibly be racist against white people. As Morehouse College Professor Dr. Marc Lamont-Hill said last year, "black people don't have the institutional power to be racist or to deploy racism."

There's only one problem with this notion: It's racist.

Racism bolstered by power is obviously more dangerous than racism without it. But racism can be used to achieve power, too—generally through the polarization of racial groups against one another. Tribalism is a powerful force, and resorting to a victimhood mentality to explain tribalism away doesn't make it any less toxic. The faster Americans learn that, the faster racism can actually be curbed rather than exacerbated.

The Unbridgeable Gap Between Left and Right Over Human Evil

June 7, 2017

There are certain clarifying moments in political discourse; moments that demonstrate just where the various parties stand. Never has the gap been so obvious as this last week. On Friday, the left declared the world in imminent peril. The problem? President Trump pulled out of the altogether meaningless Paris climate accord, a worldwide agreement requesting nonbinding commitments from signatories about future carbon emissions cuts. The hysteria was palpable. Suddenly, debunked weather prognosticator Al Gore found himself in prime television slots jabbering about the end of the world. House Minority Leader Nancy Pelosi gabbled about how Trump was "dishonoring" God (no word on her abortion-on-demand position from the Holy One—blessed be he). The Huffington Post ran a headline showing the world in flames. The mayor of London, Sadiq Khan, released a statement bemoaning Trump's decision.

Meanwhile, the right shrugged. It pointed out that the agreement did virtually nothing anyway; that it did not bind China and India to any serious commitments; that the Senate had not passed any enabling legislation; and that perhaps nongovernment alternatives should be considered before diving headlong into empowerment of the regulatory state to fight a rising temperature over the next century.

On Saturday, a group of Islamic terrorists drove a van into a crowd on the London Bridge, and then jumped out of the vehicle and began stabbing people in surrounding establishments. The Islamic State group claimed responsibility. The right immediately labeled the attacks yet another example of Islamic extremism on the march, linking them with the Manchester terror attack. President Trump immediately took to Twitter to denounce the terror attacks and call for an end to politically correct policies, as well as to stump for his travel ban. Conservatives on both sides of the Atlantic complained about leftist multiculturalism creating room for Islamic terror growth.

Meanwhile, the left shrugged. Sally Kohn tweeted about the glories of political correctness. Paul Krugman compared being killed in a terrorist attack to being killed by a drunk driver. Democrats complained about President Trump's attacks on Khan, who was busy urging Londoners to stay calm after panicking about global warming just days ago.

What explains the gap between right and left?

The left believes that human beings are inherently good, and that only environment defines whether they will act in evil fashion. That's why Sen. Bernie Sanders articulated in 2016 that global warming was the spur to terrorism; it's why the Obama administration routinely suggested that poverty caused terrorism. External circumstances dictate the morality of individual actors. That's also why the left argues we shouldn't hold people responsible for their actions as a general rule; instead, we should reshape society.

The right believes that human beings are capable of evil on their own. That's why they see the rise of radical Islam as more of a problem than global warming. Good people won't kill each other because of global warming. They will if they begin to believe evil ideologies, or support those who do.

This gap isn't bridgeable. It goes to the nature of humanity and our perception of that nature. But it's requiring a greater and greater strain these days to blame anybody but individual human beings in free Western societies for their own descent into evil.

Why the Left Protects Islam

July 26, 2017

Richard Dawkins is no friend to conservatives. The atheist author has spent much of his life deriding Judaism and Christianity. He once stated, "An atheist is just somebody who feels about Yahweh the way any decent Christian feels about Thor or Baal or the golden calf." Dawkins says that even moderate religious people "make the world safe for extremists." He's far to the left on politics: He's pro-abortion rights, and a supporter of the Labour Party and the Liberal Democrats in Britain.

But he's also smart enough to recognize that radical Islam is a greater threat to human life than Christianity or Judaism. He explains: "I have criticised the appalling misogyny and homophobia of Islam, I have criticised the murdering of apostates for no crime other than their disbelief. ... Muslims themselves are the prime victims of the oppressive cruelties of Islamism."

Such language makes him a pariah among leftists.

This week, Dawkins was scheduled to speak at an event with KPFA radio in Berkeley, California. All went swimmingly—until leftists realized that Dawkins had said some untoward things about Islam. The station then canceled the event, citing his "abusive speech." It explained: "We had booked this event based entirely on his excellent new book on science, when we didn't know he had offended and hurt—in his tweets and other comments on Islam, so many people. KPFA does not endorse hurtful speech."

This is no shock. The same left that barred Dawkins from his Berkeley event cheered this week while Palestinian Arabs rioted over metal detectors at the Temple Mount. Those leftists proclaim that the true obstacle to peace in the Middle East isn't Palestinian Arab violence—it isn't Palestinians who stab Israeli Druz officers on the Temple Mount; or the Palestinians who invade homes and slaughter old men and women; or the Palestinians in government who cheer, honor and financially support such behavior. No, the problem is the Jews.

The same left that blames metal detectors for murderous assaults and Richard Dawkins for offending Islam makes excuses for radical Muslim and Women's March on Washington organizer Linda Sarsour, who has called for certain apostate Muslims to have their genitals removed, says that Zionists cannot be feminists and stands up for terrorists and terror supporters.

Why does the left seek to support radical Islam so ardently? Because the left believes that the quickest way to destroy Western civilization is no longer class warfare but multicultural warfare: Simply ally with groups that hate the prevailing system and work with them to take it down. Then, the left will build on the ashes of the old system. In this view, Dawkins is an opponent—how can the left recruit Muslims to fight the system if Dawkins is busy alienating them? They support the Palestinian terror regime—how can that colonialist outpost, Israel, be defeated without a little blood? They applaud Sarsour—she's an ally, so she must be backed.

Alliance with nefarious forces calls your own morality into question. KPFA has a lot more to answer for than Dawkins. But the left will never have to answer such questions so long as it focuses in on its common enemy: a supposedly conservative establishment that must be fought with any tool at its disposal.

America's Left in the Grip of Insanity

January 3, 2018

President Trump is unpopular. He's unpopular because he's boorish, crude and silly; he's unpopular because he has a unique capacity to turn winning news cycles into referenda on his use of Twitter. But the United States under President Trump hasn't seen any serious anti-liberty revanchism. In fact, under Trump, regulations have dropped precipitously; the economy continues its pattern of growth; and press freedoms have actually been strengthened. Despite popular opinion, women aren't on the verge of enslavement into Vice President Mike Pence's "Handmaid's Tale," nor are black Americans in danger of resegregation or political disenfranchisement.

Yet while Iranians protest against a regime that reportedly hangs homosexuals from cranes, members of the hard left in the United States insist that protesters against the Trump administration demonstrate bravery similar to that of Iranians risking death by an Islamist regime. Huffington Post political commentator Alex Mohajer tweeted: "The #IranianProtests, the #Resistance, and @WomensMarch are all the same. Across the world, people are fighting autocracies and oppressive regimes. @realDonaldTrump is NO DIFFERENT than the oppressive Ayatollahs in Iran." Oddly, that movement of solidarity hasn't prompted those who walked in the Women's March on Washington to say a single word in support of the Iranian protesters to this point.

This idiocy doesn't merely spring from hatred for Trump but from a deep-seated need to justify the Obama administration's feckless Iran policy. Thomas Erdbrink of The New York Times reported that violence broke out in Iran after the demonstrators ignored "pleas for calm from President Hassan Rouhani" and termed Rouhani—a tool of the mullahs—a "moderate." Meanwhile, one

CNN anchor fretted that Trump might put a "finger on the scale" against the Iranian regime. Members of the Obama administration took to Twitter to tell Trump to be quiet (Susan Rice, former national security adviser), chide Trump for failing to take in Iranian refugees (Samantha Power, former U.N. ambassador) and suggest that American policy has nothing to do with Iran's protests (Ben Rhodes, former national security adviser and architect of the Iran nuclear deal narrative). All of these administration members did nothing as President Obama watched dissidents die in the streets in 2009, and all of them actively abetted the maximization of Iran's regional power.

Herein lies the insanity of the left. Only nutcases on the right believed that Barack Obama's governance was morally equivalent to the Iranian government. In the main, conservatives thought that Obama pursued bad policies domestically and horribly immoral foreign policies. But many on the left seem to believe that Trump is merely steps removed from the ayatollahs. The ayatollahs agree, and they use that nuttery for public-relations leverage: No wonder Ayatollah Khamenei tweeted: "The U.S. gov. commits oppression inside the U.S., too. U.S. police murder black women, men, & children for no justifiable reason, and the murderers are acquitted in U.S. courts. This is their judicial system! And they slam other countries' and our country's judicial system. #BLM."

Trump isn't Khamenei. And the only recent administration to help build Iran's power is the Obama administration. Comparing the Trump administration to Iran's regime isn't just delusional; it's insulting and counterproductive. And the only people it helps are America's enemies.

If You Don't Agree With Me, You're a Racist Who Likes Death Threats

April 18, 2018

On Monday, George Yancy, a black professor of philosophy at Emory University, wrote a lengthy piece in The New York Times detailing the awful death threats he has received from white racists. I can sympathize—throughout 2016, I received my fair share of death threats. But Yancy sees those death threats as representative of a deeper malignancy plaguing all of white America, not a sickness within a subset of the population. Thus, he asks, "Should I Give up on White People?"

Yancy's case isn't particularly strong.

According to him, he faces a serious dilemma: "Do I give up on white people, on white America, or do I continue to fight for a better white America, despite the fact that my efforts continue to lead to forms of unspeakable white racist backlash?" But why exactly is that a serious dilemma? America isn't filled with racists—America is one of the least racist places on Earth, and its rate of racism has been decreasing steadily for years. In order for Yates' complaint to make any sense, he has to believe that America is actually becoming *more* racist.

And he does. He says that he is "convinced that America suffers from a pervasively malignant and malicious systemic illness—white racism." He offers no statistics to support this contention. And he suggests that those who disagree with his contention do so out of willingness to ignore white racism: "There is also an appalling lack of courage, weakness of will, spinelessness and indifference in our country that helps to sustain it."

So, to get this straight, you may not be racist, but if you believe that most Americans aren't racist, just like you, you're an aider and abettor of racism. You're in league with those sending the death threats. In fact, you're a monster under almost any circumstances. Yancy calls white Americans "monsters ... Land takers. Brutal dispossession. And then body snatchers and the selling and buying of black flesh." No one alive in the United States has forcibly dispossessed anyone of land; this has been true for generations. No one alive in the United States has been involved in the slave trade. Yet the legacy of white racism lives on in us, according to Yancy.

So, how are white Americans to escape this label?

Only by agreeing with Yancy. He praises one of his white students who agreed: "The system is racist. As a white woman, I am responsible to dismantle that system as well as the attitudes in me that growing up in the system created. I am responsible for speaking out when I hear racist comments."

Well, of course we're responsible for speaking out when we hear racist comments. That's not a revelation. But Yancy wants more than that. He wants a collective oath by white people to never deny generalized white racism, fact-free or not.

Which, of course, is racist. Yes, racism plays a central role in American history. Yes, there are still racists in America. But slandering white America in general for the crimes of a few bad apples is no better than slandering black America for the crimes of a few. If Yancy wants to deal with racist death threats, he could start by recognizing that we're all in this together—and that we side with him against those who threaten him—rather than pre-emptively characterizing us as the types of people who would write such vitriolic and evil screeds.

The Left's War on Parenting

December 19, 2018

Last month, the New York State Education Department made a crucial decision: Commissioner MaryEllen Elia handed authority to local school boards to veto the right for private schools to operate. Those school boards must now determine whether private schools provide an education "substantially equivalent to that received in district public schools." According to Jewish educators Elya Brudny and Yisroel Reisman, "The state government now requires private schools to offer a specific set of classes more comprehensive than what students in public schools must learn." This isn't a problem for Jewish schools alone—Catholic schools in New York have bucked the legislation, with James Cultrara, executive secretary of the New York Council of Catholic School Superintendents, explaining, "We simply cannot accept a competing school having authority over whether our schools can operate."

Now there's a case to be made that the state has an interest in children learning basic secular studies, and to that end, Cultrara has called for an objective standard for evaluating whether or not schools are properly educating their students. That case is far stronger in a welfare state, in which insufficient education often ends with the public bearing the brunt of such failures.

But there's also a case to be made that parents are the best sources for judging which educational standards their children should obtain—and that attempting to force-feed education to unwilling students and parents at threat of legal peril is a massive imposition on freedom. It's also unlikely that a broadly applied standard of education will succeed in raising standards across the board. The public school system hasn't been able to achieve that even absent religious conflicts.

More fascinating than this debate, however, is the generalized attitude toward parenting expressed by the social left. If you choose to send your child to a non-approved yeshiva, you must be policed and your child threatened with truancy. If, however, you are a parent who decides to expose your 11-year-old son to risk of sexual perversion, then you're open-minded and noble.

What else are we to take from the story of Desmond Napoles? Napoles is an 11-year-old boy who dresses in drag for national press, and who was squired—presumably by his parents—to a gay bar in Brooklyn, New York, called 3 Dollar Bill, where grown men proceeded to hand dollar bills to him. As writer Matt Walsh has pointed out, were Desmond a girl being paraded by her parents before the leering stares of grown men, child protective services would be called. But since Desmond is a celebrity who has been exploited by his parents, this is all worth celebrating.

Which is, perhaps, one of the reasons so many religious parents don't want the state of New York determining what they should and should not be allowed to teach their children. Religious parents may look at the world created by the social left and say that they want to inculcate in their children an alternative set of values. There may be costs to that. Perhaps there are ways to mitigate those costs. But overall, only one set of parents is being punished for making "educational" decisions by the state of New York—and it's not the set of parents cross-dressing their pre-pubescent children for fun and cash.

SOAPBOX: Culture

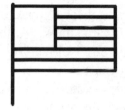

*America was established not to create wealth but to realize a vision,
to realize an ideal - to discover and maintain liberty among men.*
—Woodrow Wilson

How America Lost Its Head

May 31, 2017

In 2013, the left went nuts over a rodeo clown.

The rodeo clown was performing at the Missouri State Fair, and he had the awful temerity to wear a mask of then-President Obama. "We're going to stomp Obama now," said an announcer. "Hey, I know I'm a clown," the rodeo clown replied. "He's just running around acting like one. Doesn't know he is one." The media quoted a bystander who compared the act to a Ku Klux Klan rally. The lieutenant governor of the state condemned the act, as did one of the senators. The rodeo clown was fired, even though he'd dressed up as other presidents in the past.

Fast-forward four years.

On Tuesday, TMZ posted photos of comedienne Kathy Griffin, who has helped host CNN's New Year's Eve coverage for a decade, holding a mock-up of President Trump's severed head covered in blood. Griffin has a long record of anti-Trump sentiment, of course; in February, she told MSNBC's Chris Matthews: "I'm a big resister, and I don't believe in compromise with this president. I also think he's crazy. I think he's mentally ill. He's also an idiot." But this photo shoot crossed a rather obvious line—it celebrated Trump's prospective murder. Imagine if anyone on the right had done something similar with Obama. The outcry would have been deafening.

Yet the same people who ask for trigger warnings for material that might offend anyone; the same people who believe that there is a "rape culture" that pervades America; the same people who say that President Trump has incentivized a culture of political violence across the land; are largely silent about Griffin's antics. Why? Because political violence is no longer taboo in the United States.

It's just another tactic to utilize when useful and denigrate when others engage in it.

That sentiment expresses itself on both sides of the political aisle. When Montana House candidate Greg Gianforte allegedly body-slammed a reporter, prominent conservatives including talk-show host Laura Ingraham demeaned his victim as a wuss and championed Gianforte as a sort of stalwart man's man. When leftists attacked Trump rallies during the 2016 election cycle, the media attempted to paint them as defenders of the common good against Trump himself.

The overused phrase "cycle of violence" is often used by the press to refer to situations in which an aggressor acts violently and somebody defends him. But we've entered an actual cycle in violent political rhetoric, whereby the vileness of the left provokes a direct response from the right, and vice versa.

And it's getting worse.

If you spend all day proclaiming that you're in a "civil war" with other Americans, that you're part of the "resistance," it's only a matter of time until you become willing to look the other way at violence itself. If Americans aren't your brothers and sisters, if we disagree, then they will quickly become your enemies. Kathy Griffin may think it's hilarious to hold up a bloody head of the president of the United States, but she's tearing away at the social fabric far more than President Trump. And those who back her play are helping to provoke their enemies to respond in kind.

On 'Muh Principles'

June 21, 2017

"Muh principles."

It's a phrase we hear over and over on Twitter whenever someone criticizes morally troubling anti-leftist tactics used by members of the right. They say: "What are you, some sort of coward? What, are you worried about muh principles?" The phrase is meant to deride the supposed moral preening of those who criticize—they must think themselves high and mighty, whining about virtue where some good hard-nosed old-fashioned get-in-the-dirt-and-fight-'em tactics would do. Those worries about right and wrong just hamstring the right. "Muh principles" are a liability. Why can't those weaklings just get over their supposed moral purity and fight in the trenches?

Now, I'm no fan of political cowardice. I wrote an entire book called "Bullies," in which I blasted the left's character assassination techniques. I routinely speak on college campuses in conditions that are less than physically secure. I'm more than happy to tell people things they don't want to hear in political debate, and I've been threatened more than once for my trouble.

But I'm a fan of principles.

I'm a fan of principles because without them, politics becomes meaningless. Even those who criticize "muh principles" have their own principles. The "muh principles" crowd's highest principle is supposedly defeating the left. That is its entire argument: If you stick with your wishy-washy principles about civility, you'll lose! And if you lose, my principles will be destroyed!

But, as it turns out, many of those who mock "muh principles" have no actual principles other than empty tribal victory. Never was that clearer than this week when several of the self-appointed members of the Trump-ardent defense squad went full social justice warrior, invading a Shakespeare in the Park performance of "Julius Caesar" that depicts President Trump as Caesar. Screaming "Liberal hate kills!" they stormed the stage, called audience members Joseph Goebbels and held up the production. Those who objected to this obtuse behavior were simply being hamstrung by "muh principles," they then proclaimed.

Except that there were no principles at stake here. What was the supposed principle? Perhaps it was that artists shouldn't make art that invokes images of violence inflicted on a president. Then why weren't they upset about a rodeo clown dressed up as President Obama in 2013? Perhaps it was that radical rhetoric leads to violence. Then why weren't they upset when candidate Trump urged his followers to clock protesters? Perhaps it was that shutting down others' free speech is bad—a sort of ironic lesson for the left. Then why didn't they say so, rather than claiming that the content of the play justified their activity? And why would this be a good strategy, given that the self-immolating hard left's free speech shutdowns have backfired so dramatically that even Obama and Sens. Elizabeth Warren and Bernie Sanders have been forced to condemn them?

No, there were no principles here, other than tribalistic anti-left foolishness.

Unfortunately, that seems to be the order of the day for a few on the right. I'm old enough to remember when the pro-Trump right justified Trump's behavior on the grounds that he had to build a wall and rescind Obama's executive amnesty. Now only Ann Coulter has the guts to point out that Trump hasn't done either—and that he just enshrined for all time Obama's executive amnesty. I'm old enough to remember when the pro-Trump right assured conservatives that it would hold Trump to account if he were to fail to repeal Obamacare. Now it's ignoring the fact that he called a watered-down Obamacare too "mean" and pushed for a broader funding regime. Where are their principles? I thought "muh principles" had to go so that they could achieve theirs. But they seem rather blithe about the collapse of some of their supposed core precepts, which suggests that maybe there are some on the right who just want to fight, and have forgotten why they fight—and how to fight. All that matters now is winning, even if they have no idea what winning looks like other than the other guy losing.

Yes, Politics Is Dirty. No, It Isn't As Dirty As You Think It Is

July 19, 2017

Expectations define behavior.

The success of a marriage nearly always depends on the expectations of the parties going in. If you believe marriage is going to be a rose garden of happy trips to the beach interspersed with moonlight dinners and foot massages, you're more likely to end up cheating on your spouse when that doesn't materialize. If you believe marriage is a mechanism for changing your potential spouse, you're likely to end up estranged. If you believe that marriage is about a lifelong union devoted to self-improvement and the creation and rearing of children, you're likely to make decisions that lead to that outcome.

The same is true in politics.

Americans don't trust politicians. That's for good reason. Politicians fib to get elected; they pander to particular constituencies; they leave principle at the door in favor of convenience in order to maintain power and position. But they do not, at least not that often, murder people and collude with foreign governments.

But thanks to popular culture, that's exactly what many Americans think politicians do. If you watch "House of Cards," you're likely to believe that top-level politicians off each other on a regular basis—and you might be more willing to believe conspiracy theories about the murder of former Democratic National Committee staffer Seth Rich. If you've seen "The Manchurian Candidate," you're more likely to believe that either former President Obama or President Trump is one.

President Trump, who was a layman until he became president, obviously believes a lot of the pop culture mythology surrounding politics. That's why he told Bill O'Reilly that it's not that big a deal that Russian President Vladimir Putin kills his political opponents. "You think our country's so innocent?" he said in jaw-dropping fashion. That's why Trump believes that politics is such a "dirty business"—dirtier, even, than Manhattan real estate, where Trump worked with mafia figures. Politics, in Trump's mind, is the lowest of the low.

That means a more corrupt administration. If you believe, as Trump assuredly does, that anybody would take a meeting with Russian government figures to dig up dirt on an opponent, then you'll do it, too. Why be martyred just because you were too holy to get down in the mud? If you think that Hillary Clinton is the way politics is done—we shouldn't be outraged because she's just another politician—then why not play by the same rules?

Voters like to believe, as Trump does, that politics is filthy, because we refuse to acknowledge that in a representative republic, we're the ultimate sources of blame. We keep electing these moral idiots. We keep voting for them, demanding that they give us things and suggesting that they've "sold out" if they don't. We're the ones who decry crony capitalism while complaining that the local factory will leave unless the government "does something."

Politicians like to believe, as Trump does, that politics is sordid, because that's a tailor-made excuse for participating in bad behavior. It's also an excuse for legislating morality, as Sen. John McCain tried to do with campaign finance reform—you can use the public distrust of politicians to restrict the political speech of citizens, all in the name of "cleaning up the system."

It's always easier to shift our vision of politics than to shift our vision of ourselves.

And so, we get the politics we deserve. Our belief that politics is a squalid affair finds realization in our politicians, who reflect that view; and in ourselves, as we vote for those politicians. And then we're surprised when politics seems to grow more and more disreputable.

'Raising Awareness' Isn't Helping Much

October 18, 2017

"Awareness must be raised."

"A spotlight must be brought to this crucial issue."

"We must all think about our own culpability."

These tired nostrums are repeatedly deployed in our politics to explain why someone complains about a broad problem or tells a specific story of victimization without accompanying evidence that would allow us to act. Accusations of institutional racism rarely come along with specific allegations regarding specific police officers. If allegations and names were included, we could all look at the evidence and determine whether or not to call for consequences. Stories of sexual assault and harassment at work are often told without naming names. If those names were named, authorities could investigate; the media could begin collecting data; and we could do something about it.

But that would be useful. We don't want useful measures. We want to note how terrible things are generally.

Why?

What drives us to ignore the obvious fact that most Americans oppose specific evils and would side against those evils when presented with evidence of them occurring?

Perhaps it's our innate drive toward establishing a feeling of moral superiority. You don't get to feel morally superior when you name someone who acts in criminal fashion; you're just a witness, and witnesses are useful members of society, bettering society actively rather than criticizing it from the outside.

Or perhaps it's the burden that comes along with evidence. It's much easier to gain sympathy by telling a story about victimization without naming names—a story nobody can contradict, since you're not getting specific. In fact, if you *do* get too specific about allegations of sexual assault, as actress Lena Dunham did, your allegations might be called into question. And if you *do* get too specific about allegations of police racism and brutality, as the Seattle Seahawks defensive end Michael Bennett did, your accusations might be debunked.

So, is it worthwhile to complain about generalized problems without providing specific instances upon which we can agree and against which we can fight? Only on a marginal level—and in some ways, it's actually tremendously counterproductive. It may be useful to "raise awareness" among police officers about being careful in their procedures so as not to be accused of racism, for example. It may be useful to "raise awareness" among men in offices about being careful around female employees so as not to be accused of harassment. But it may also be counterproductive to rage against the system generally because it leads to false and widespread perceptions that *all* police officers are cursed with the original sin of racism, or that *all* men are cursed with "toxic masculinity."

So, here's an idea: Let's all call out bad action when we see it and be as specific as possible about it. We can all agree on what a bad guy looks like; there isn't much debate about Harvey Weinstein. But if we continue to promote the importance of "raising awareness" rather than providing evidence, our groundless distrust for one another is bound to grow and metastasize.

On the Super Bowl and the Social Fabric

February 7, 2018

On Sunday, I attended the Super Bowl, along with my father, my business partner and the president of our company. It was an amazing event. That wasn't just because the game was terrific—although it was. It was because for all the competitive fire, for all the passion and excitement, one feeling permeated the stadium in the freezing wilds of Minnesota: love.

Yes, love.

The people in the stadium may have hated the other team, but they didn't hate one another. Patriots fans sat next to Eagles fans, and everybody got along; we all shouted ourselves hoarse when the NFL honored Medal of Honor winners, and we all stood for the national anthem. After the game, when we poured out into the arctic temperatures, barely able to move because of the throng, nobody was pushing or shoving or getting violent. Instead, people joked and laughed. After all, what was there to be truly angry about? We'd just witnessed an awesome spectacle, been party to a shared communal experience. Eagles fans mocked Pats fans; Pats fans good-naturedly shrugged it off. It may sound like a cliche, but the Super Bowl—in the stadium, at least—was just a giant party filled with Americans who loved being in America celebrating a great American cultural celebration.

Unfortunately, such experiences are becoming rarer and rarer.

I love technology; I love choice. I cut cable years ago. Then I hooked up cable again for sports and then cut it again. My entertainment choices are personalized. So are my music choices. I can download podcasts at will. I watch movies with my wife—it takes a Big Event Movie to get me to a theater. I choose whom to follow on Facebook and Twitter. All of that is fantastic—better stuff, faster, catered to my tastes! But there's a drawback: We don't have the same common cultural ground anymore, as our tastes fragment and we can pursue them more individually.

My main communal connection comes through my synagogue, but church and synagogue attendance has been dropping precipitously for years. People aren't joining sports leagues or community organizations. We're fragmenting on nearly every level. There's a problem with that: As the social fabric atomizes, we spend less time with one another. We're less likely to see one another as friends and neighbors, and more likely to see one another as bundles of positions and views we don't share. And that makes it particularly easy for us to dismiss one another as motivated by nefarious feelings, as opposed to merely being in disagreement.

Arthur Brooks of American Enterprise Institute is fond of citing a 1934 study about discrimination against Chinese-Americans. The study followed a Chinese couple as they visited hotels and restaurants across the country. They were denied service a grand total of one time. Then, study author Richard LaPiere sent questionnaires to the various establishments asking whether they'd serve a Chinese couple. All but one that responded said no.

The lesson, as Brooks notes: "People are more hostile to others in the abstract than when they meet them in person." That means we need more communal events—and that means we have to go out of our way to engage with others. We need more shared cultural experiences. That would be a good start toward rebuilding our perceptions of one another.

Do Politics Matter?

August 22, 2018

This week, I bought my wife a present for her birthday: a glass-blowing class. The teacher was, predictably, an eclectically artistic type in Los Angeles, and a down-the-line liberal. As with most conversations these days, the talk turned to President Trump. She quickly let me know her opinion of him (it wasn't high); she then turned to bashing Vice President Mike Pence and Senate Majority Leader Mitch McConnell.

Not once did she raise a policy consideration. Virtually every statement revolved around her personal characterization of political actors—as good people, bad people or indifferent.

I don't think she's out of the mainstream.

There seem to be two main factors in the United States when it comes to voting. Neither has much to do with policy. The first factor is party identification: We tend to vote for the party that shares certain basic policy preferences. The second factor is personal likability of a candidate: We take into account whether we like a candidate or not. Now, these two factors are intertwined: If we like a particular candidate an awful lot, we're likely to identify more with the party of that candidate, and vice versa. This means that a milquetoast candidate's top support number will be the top support number of the party, since the party defines the candidate more than the candidate defines the party (e.g. Mitt Romney). Conversely, a bigger-than-life candidate whose personality seems untethered to the party can lift or drag down the entire party.

That's particularly true with Donald Trump. In today's political environment, your feelings about Trump actually have an impact on how people feel about *you*. Among many conservatives, your support for Trump marks you as a hard-nosed patriot; you're willing to go any distance to defeat the left. If you're among liberals and moderates, your support for Trump marks you as a scurrilous ne'er-do-well who's beneath contempt; you're willing to greenlight any vile behavior so long as you get what you want.

In red or blue districts, this may not matter. But in purple districts, it does. If you have friends on the other side of the aisle, it's uncomfortable to defend Trump's excesses and idiocies. That makes you less likely to openly support Trump, and less likely to support the Republican Party in congressional elections. Presidents who make it difficult to defend them depress turnout in swing districts.

All of which means that if President Trump truly cares about retaining Congress, he has to stop thinking about his base and start thinking about those in the competitive districts. How can he make their lives easier? That's not about policy. At the very least, it's about generating fewer headlines. Trump's base is rock-solid, and it's not going anywhere. But he needs more than his base to win in 2018 and 2020. And barring a personality change, that means minimizing the transaction costs of defending him for those who must show up to the polls.

What Nonreligious People Get Wrong About Religious People

August 29, 2018

With the media furiously obsessed over the supposed imminent end of the Trump presidency (spoiler alert: nope), the new conversation among the elite concerns the supposed evils of Vice President Mike Pence. Pence, our leftist thought leaders proclaim, is perhaps even more frightening than President Trump. Frank Bruni of The New York Times terms Pence a "holy terror waiting in the wings ... a bigot ... a liar ... cruel."

This is nothing new. Conan O'Brien says that "many members of Congress are preparing for a Mike Pence presidency. Yeah, they're preparing by binge-watching 'The Handmaid's Tale.'" Joy Behar called Pence's faith a "mental illness." John Oliver trolled Pence last year by mocking his daughter's children's book about a bunny rabbit -- in Oliver's parody book, the bunny rabbit is gay. Because, of course, Pence would *hate* a gay bunny.

Last year, the media went into a tizzy when they learned that Pence refuses to dine alone with women other than his wife (the same media have since been shocked to learn that Harvey Weinstein *loved* dining alone with women other than his wife). This policy made Pence a bigot. But that was just the beginning. Pence, said the media, supported "gay conversion therapy." This, of course, is false as well. But that didn't stop the media from feting gay 2018 Winter Olympian Adam Rippon, who proceeded to trot out that debunked chestnut.

What is so frightening about Pence? His status as a religious Christian. According to many on the left, Pence's religiosity means he's a theocrat. Never mind the fact that Pence is a limited-government conservative who isn't generally interested in imposing policy preferences from above; he believes in The Jesus, and therefore, he must want to install himself at the head of the United Christian States of America.

But that isn't even what bothers those on the left. What bothers many on the left about Pence is the same thing that bothers them about religious Christians in general: They seem convinced that religious Americans are merely bigots hiding behind the Bible. The perspective is well-expressed by Greg Carey, professor of the New Testament at Lancaster Theological Seminary: "People either use religion to justify their bigotry or they refuse to give up their bigotry for the sake of maintaining false religious security." Or let's listen to Bruni again, this time from April 2015: "our debate about religious freedom should include a conversation about freeing religions and religious people from prejudices that they needn't cling to." Or Hillary Clinton in 2016: "deep-seated cultural codes, religious beliefs and structural biases have to be changed."

This view of religious belief is deeply demeaning. The suggestion seems to be that religious texts are utterly malleable, and that human beings twist them to fit their preconceived notions. But the suggestion is alien to most religious people, who believe that their religion dictates and they listen. This perception gap plagues our public discourse and helps explain why the left seems so unperturbed by violating the religious-practice rights of other Americans: They think those Americans are bad human beings using the Bible to shield themselves. Pence is merely the latest example.

The great irony, of course, is that religious people generally wish to be left alone. They're not seeking to impose "The Handmaid's Tale"; such compulsion is endemic to a left that insists we "bake the cake." Such psychological projection damages the public discourse and undermines cultural unity. If the left truly wants a more tolerant America, perhaps it should start by assuming that its opponents in the religious community aren't mere bigots cloaked in the vestments of God—and perhaps it ought to think more deeply about whether the true bigotry lies within itself.

What Do We Have In Common?

October 10, 2018

America stands at a precipice.

It's a moral precipice of our own making: We're not facing any external existential threat, or any serious economic crisis. Nonetheless, we're at each other's throats in a shocking and unique way. At least in the 1960s, serious issues divided us: the national attempt to grapple with legally enshrined racism, the sexual revolution, the Vietnam War. We have no such excuse now. Yet to view the sheer chaos surrounding the confirmation of Justice Brett Kavanaugh is to realize that we may simply have nothing in common anymore, other than our sheer blind luck at having been born into the most prosperous, free, productive country in world history.

But a nation is more than a country. A nation is a people united by history, ideals, culture, institutions. But we've been steadily chipping away at each element of that nationhood.

Our history now divides us. This week, retired astronaut Scott Kelly was forced to apologize on Twitter for the grave sin of quoting Winston Churchill; he tweeted, "I will go and educate myself further on his atrocities, racist views which I do not support." Meanwhile, across America, left-leaning city councils celebrated Indigenous Peoples Day in place of Columbus Day, signaling their belief that Christopher Columbus' discovery of the New World was a tragedy rather than a cause for celebration. We Americans are in the midst of a serious division regarding our own character: Was America and the West founded on fundamentally good and eternal principles, principles we've sometimes failed to live up to, of course, but principles worth fighting for? Or is America and the West the font of evil, the source of suffering, and is all our prosperity merely the fruit of the poisonous tree?

Our ideals divide us, too. On the one hand are "red state" Americans, steeped in traditional Judeo-Christian principles and mores—Americans who believe that our rights are God-given, and that liberty must be balanced by traditional moral virtue. On the other hand are "blue state" Americans, steeped in egalitarian principles and mores—Americans who believe that rights spring from government, and that inequality is a more pressing concern than individual liberty, and that systems of traditional virtue merely mask hierarchical power structures.

Without a shared history or shared ideals, culture and institutions crumble. Our culture has fragmented - can we celebrate July Fourth and stand for the national anthem together, or even watch a football game without arguing about our divisions? Can we attend a movie together without feeling sandbagged by the questions that divide us outside the theater? We certainly no longer attend church or even go bowling together.

And as for institutions, Democrats have now discussed packing the Supreme Court, destroying the Senate and ending the Electoral College thanks to their recent spate of political defeats. All of that follows hard on former President Barack Obama simply arrogating power to himself when he couldn't get Congress to go along with him. Our institutions won't restrain us if we decide to tear ourselves apart.

So, what can hold us together? We can start with gratitude, gratitude for this unique moment in human history, for our unique country, for our unique ideals, for our unique institutions. If we're ungrateful, spite will win the day. And that means that we could be setting the charges for a spectacular implosion.

Why Celebrity Politics Matters

June 5, 2019

This week, celebrities emerged from their Hollywood cocoon to sound off on abortion law ... in Georgia. If this sounds bizarre, that's because it is: The people of Georgia don't spend an awful lot of time trying to control the policies of New York or California. Yet the greatest and most moral among us—people who read lines for a living and look attractive for magazine covers—now lecture people thousands of miles away on the necessity of late-term abortion.

Netflix led the charge, announcing that it might cease filming in the state of Georgia should the state impose its "heartbeat bill," protecting the lives of the unborn from the sixth week of pregnancy. Netflix is simultaneously filming in Egypt and Jordan, where abortion is heavily restricted.

Disney soon joined the club, stating that it could pull production as well. Reese Witherspoon spoke up on behalf of females everywhere, saying: "Women of Alabama, I will fight for you. Women of Georgia, I will fight for you. Women of Ohio, Kentucky, Missouri and Mississippi, I will fight for you." Never mind that majorities of women in nearly all of these states are pro-life. Witherspoon knows that *true* women support her agenda. Sophie Turner of "Game of Thrones," too, announced that she wouldn't film in Georgia—after filming her role as Sansa Stark in Northern Ireland, where abortion is illegal.

This sort of disdain of our culture's supposed elite for those who disagree politically is helping drive another wedge into our national divide. It's actually promoting a spiral of division that has severe consequences for our national polis.

Here's how it works.

Culture is supposed to be the binding glue for any nation. The United States is ethnically, politically and religiously diverse. Only a few key threads still bind citizens from New York with citizens from Georgia: symbols like the American flag, institutions like the American military and, yes, water cooler conversations over sports, movies, music and television.

The American left has politicized each of these threads, in effect fraying them. The American flag itself has become a symbol of division, as our cultural betters—and the gimlet-eyed marketing firms that power corporations like Nike—decide to glorify protests against the flag. The American military has been politicized, too, with Hollywood portraying soldiers as either victims or villains (aside from a few rarities like "American Sniper"—which, not coincidentally, did enormous in the box office). Our movies and television and music have become politicized, too, with artists deemed "unwoke" if they refuse to speak up on the issues of the day.

Conservatives have responded by first paying outsized attention to cultural figures who *don't* disdain them—see Trump, Donald— and, second, by showing up in droves to vote. If conservatives can't control the culture, they certainly can control their legislators.

Our cultural arbiters, in turn, have reacted to the political victory of their opposition with renewed attempts to merge culture and politics—they've gotten more extreme, louder, more pronounced in their determination to shift the culture to their point of view. Which will, of course, drive more political divisions.

A pluralistic democracy requires three factors to function: a shared cultural space; a shared belief in key ideas, largely embedded in the Constitution; and a shared willingness to leave one another alone. As each component erodes, so, too, does the possibility of a united country.

Anger for Anger's Sake

June 10, 2019

In the last two weeks, America has learned that a bevy of heretofore relatively uncontroversial objects and ideas are, in fact, extraordinarily controversial. We have learned that the Betsy Ross American flag is irredeemably racist. We have learned that Disney casting a black woman as Ariel in the live-action remake of "The Little Mermaid" is supposedly supremely disquieting for a racist America. We have learned that opposing federally mandated forced busing means that you are a secret bigot, so long as you are named Joe Biden.

Or perhaps we haven't learned any of those things. Perhaps all of this is nonsense, and we've merely learned that Americans are angry, that they're channeling that anger in increasingly bizarre directions, and that opportunists of every stripe are willing to take advantage of that anger for their own benefit.

Take, for example, the Betsy Ross flag. Not only was Ross an abolitionist Quaker; the flag has flown for centuries as a symbol of a country that fought the single bloodiest war in its history to abolish slavery. The flag flew at Barack Obama's inauguration. Not until the last five minutes was someone cloddish enough to suggest that the flag represents slavery and racism—until Nike announced that it had canceled the manufacture of a Ross-inspired shoe at the behest of failed NFL quarterback and national anthem kneeler Colin Kaepernick.

Kaepernick, whose knowledge of politics is approximately as accurate as his downfield passing game, apparently taught Nike some tough lessons about American history (not about sweatshop labor, however). Thus, the sneakers were withdrawn, and a weeklong controversy ensued about the supposed evils of the Ross flag.

The good news for Nike: Its stock rose. That's because Nike knows that controversy generates earned media, and it knows that black Americans are far more likely to be attracted to its social justice warrior posturing *and* more likely to buy more Nike shoes (one study from 1986 to 2002 found that blacks and Hispanics spend up to 30% more on apparel and jewelry than whites with comparable incomes).

Corporations understand that nontroversies can sell, just so long as you can sell them as controversies. When Disney announced this month that the actress playing Ariel in its live-action remake of "The Little Mermaid" is Halle Bailey, who is black, a few internet trolls tweeted #NotMyAriel. Soon, the world was aflame with news that the Disney-loving KKK was out of the woodwork; Freeform, a Disney-owned cable channel, immediately unleashed a long open letter "clapping back" at the critics, not a single one of whom was prominent enough to be named.

And in the end, that's how this works: Everyone gets credit for "clapping back," even if there was no actual clapping in the first place.

It works politically, too. The big winner from the first Democratic primary debate was Sen. Kamala Harris, D-Calif., who lumped herself in with Rosa Parks this week after bashing former Vice President Joe Biden for having failed to support federally mandated forced busing in the 1970s. When asked whether she would support such a program, Harris demurred—as, indeed, she had to, since forced busing is wildly unpopular and was wildly unsuccessful, carrying unintended consequences that actually exacerbated de facto segregation rather than alleviating it. She still got points for knocking Biden, though she holds *his exact position* on the issue.

There's a lot of profit to be made, both politically and financially, in generating and maintaining stupid controversy. Perhaps that speaks to our national need for catharsis. But here's the thing about unjustifiable anger: It's never satiated. So watch for our controversies to get stupider and stupider—and more and more profitable for those who egg them on.

SOAPBOX: Government

Let us never forget that government is ourselves and not an alien power over us. The ultimate rulers of our democracy are not a President and senators and congressmen and government officials, but the voters of this country.
—Franklin D. Roosevelt

Does Being Presidential Matter Anymore?

July 5, 2017

It's tempting to view President Trump as the end of the American presidential tradition. It's difficult to imagine George Washington pondering a future president of the United States tweeting out memes of himself clotheslining a CNN-logoed enemy. It would certainly confuse Abraham Lincoln to see the president jabbering about media enemies' bloody face-lifts and then declaring himself "modern day presidential." On moving into the White House, John Adams wrote to his wife, Abigail Adams, "May none but honest and wise Men ever rule under this roof."

Yeah, not so much.

But while the media act as though Trump is a shocking break from his predecessors, the fact is that they took the first steps down the path of merging the frivolous and the grave. They began violating public standards long before Trump was ever a presidential contender. Trump defenders aren't wrong to scoff at Bill Clinton supporters suddenly discovering presidential propriety two decades after defending their favorite's cigar tricks with a White House intern in the Oval Office. And Barack Obama wasn't exactly shy about making the media rounds in the most ridiculous way—it was he, after all, who began appearing with GloZell and Pimp With the Limp in order to press forward his political case.

But Trump is indeed something new. He doesn't even pretend to be presidential. Clinton failed at being presidential, but he still *wanted* to be seen as a serious human being; Obama tried to position himself as a serious thinker, even as he did his latest ESPN brackets. Trump has no such pretentions—or if he does, his volatile id won't allow him to stick to them. He's open and obvious about his disdain for decency and protocol. He spends his days trolling Reddit and 4chan for the latest dank memes to post to his Twitter account, and then he waits with bated breath as his followers cheer themselves hoarse.

So, does any of this matter?

It's tempting to say that it doesn't. George W. Bush attempted to restore some honor to the office after Clinton spread his bodily juices all over it. The media savaged him anyway, and called him a nincompoop and a dunce and a humiliation to the office. Obama entered on eagle's wings and promptly used the bully pulpit to attack his enemies and cover for his friends. What difference does it make whether Trump finally strips the mask off the hoity-toity old boys club that the White House represents?

Actually, it does make a difference.

It makes a difference because while we're always going to have the rough-and-tumble of politics—and we *should*, because we live in a free country—there's a whole generation of Americans who have been gradually acclimated to bad behavior by their leaders. Clinton started us down a dark path. Trump stands at the end of the path, thanks, ironically, to the public's distaste for the Clintons. Trump could have helped restore a sense of honor to the White House. He didn't. It's possible in theory that such a failure could help Americans turn to a sort of small-government libertarianism and say to themselves, "Hey, why give these dolts a bunch of power?" Instead, Americans seem to be saying to themselves: "Hey, why do the other guys get to be awful? Why can't we do it, too?"

The result: a race to the bottom. That race seems to be accelerating daily now. Again, that's not Trump's fault. It's ours. We ought to demand that our politicians be more than celebrities who enjoy WWE memes or Hollywood-adored figureheads for "woke" talking points. They ought to act out some sort of honor in their Constitutional roles. It's enough to churn the stomach to imagine the great people who once occupied the halls of power, and then consider what moral Lilliputians now roam there.

The End of the First Amendment

September 20, 2017

Last week, I visited the University of California, Berkeley.

The preparations for the visit were patently insane. First, the school charged the sponsor group, Young America's Foundation, a $15,000 security fee. Then, the school blocked off the upper level of the auditorium, fearful that radicals from the violent far-left-leaning group antifa would infiltrate the speech and begin hurling objects from the balcony onto the crowd below. Finally, the school ended up spending some $600,000 on additional policing, including the creation of cement barriers and hiring of hundreds of armed police officers for a prospective riot.

All this so that I could deliver a speech about personal responsibility and individualism.

Good for Berkeley for doing its job. Bad for the students and outside agitators who made it necessary. Unfortunately, the bad actors are becoming more prominent and more popular. At The University of Utah, we're already hearing rumors of unrest. And, according to an astonishing new survey from Brookings Institution, such idiocy is set to multiply: A full 44 percent of students said that the First Amendment does not protect "hate speech"; a majority of students, 51 percent, said that they would be in favor of students shouting down a speaker "known for making offensive and hurtful statements"; Nineteen percent of students said the use of violence against controversial speakers would be acceptable.

This is full-scale fascism, and it's gaining ground.

Meanwhile, administrators are caving. At Middlebury College, administrators have adopted a policy that explicitly states, "Only in cases of imminent and credible threat to the community that cannot be mitigated by revisions to the event plan would the president and senior administration consider canceling the event." At DePaul

University, I was pre-emptively banned from campus last year after students got violent with another speaker. At the University of Wisconsin-Madison, police left students who decided to storm the stage while I was speaking to their own devices; administrators reportedly told the police not to remove the agitators and to cancel the event if they felt it necessary to do so. At California State University, Los Angeles, administrators allegedly told police to stand down rather than fight near-rioters getting violent with those who would attend one of my speeches.

Both students and administrators should take a lesson from Berkeley.

First, administrators: Security is necessary for the free exercise of the First Amendment. Right now, there's an expectation that police will be prevented from doing their jobs; that's why groups like antifa roam free. At Berkeley, they knew better: The police were armed with pepper spray and told to arrest anyone in a mask or with a barred weapon. The result was 1,000 protesters and no serious violence. That was after months of actual brutal violence in the streets of Berkeley. Other campuses must take note.

Second, students: Get a grip. I spoke at Berkeley without incident, and we actually had productive discussions with a number of students on the left. Everybody left with more information than they had coming in. Discussion never hurt anyone. But both the heckler's veto and the fascistic worldview that fuels it do.

What Are Our Representatives Supposed to Do?

November 15, 2017

During America's founding era, a significant debate took place about the nature of representation in a democratically elected government. Were representatives supposed to act as simple proxies for their constituents? Or were they supposed to exercise independent judgment? Edmund Burke was a forceful advocate for the latter position: A representative, he said, was supposed to exercise his "mature judgment, his enlightened conscience. And "he ought not to sacrifice to you, to any man, or to any set of men living." John Stuart Mill, too, believed that representatives ought to act independently; he said: "A person whose desires and impulses are his own...is said to have a character. One whose desires and impulses are not his own, has no character, no more than a steam-engine has a character."

Then there were those who argued that to exercise independent judgment would be to betray voters, that they sent you there with a mission, and your job is to fulfill that mission. This so-called delegate view of representation is supremely transactional—we only bother electing representatives in this view in order to do the work we're not willing to do. They aren't elected to spend time learning about the issues or broaden their perspective beyond the regional. They're there to do what you want them to do.

This debate has finally come to a head recently, not because sectional representatives have forgone their voters but because characterless people are running for office more and more. Those who believe in the Burkean model oppose such people—we say that to put those without character in charge of policy is to leave our future in the hands of the untrustworthy. Those who believe in the delegate model can embrace such people—they say that so long as the representative votes the right way on the issues, they can murder dogs in the backyard or allegedly molest young girls. Nina Burleigh's perspective on then-President Bill Clinton falls into this second camp. "I would be happy to give him a blow job just to thank him for keeping abortion legal," she said. So does Rep. Mo Brooks' perspective on Alabama Republican Senate candidate Roy Moore. He said: "Roy Moore will vote right ... That's why I'm voting for Roy Moore."

There's a certain freedom to this perspective. It allows us to forgo discussion about the nature of the people we support—so long as they're not lying about how they vote, we can trust them in office. The founders, however, would have rejected this perspective. The Federalist Papers are replete with explanations of just why a good government would require good men. The founders greatly feared the constraints of a parchment barrier against characterless men; they didn't trust human nature enough to believe that child molesters or puppy torturers would be bound by simple conformity with the public will.

And the founders were right. History has shown that bad men in positions of power rarely get better; they often get worse. They tend to abuse power. They tend to exercise their judgment—or lack thereof—even when they pledge to do otherwise. That means that we must measure our candidates for character as well as position. "May none but honest and wise men ever rule under this roof," President John Adams prayed regarding the White House. He didn't pray that they agree with him on tariffs.

What the Latest Stupid Government Shutdown Means

January 24, 2018

On Monday, Democrats caved on their manufactured government shutdown. In an attempt to generate a groundswell of support for a legislative re-enshrinement of former President Obama's executive amnesty, Democrats filibustered a continuing resolution to fund the government. That tough stance lasted precisely three days. Then, Democrats voted overwhelmingly with Republicans to fund the government in its entirety for another three weeks.

This makes the second government shutdown in the last five years; back in 2013, the Republicans refused to fund then-President Obama's Affordable Care Act and then collapsed and fully funded it for nothing in return. That followed a government shutdown in 1995-1996 that ended after nearly a month, with Republicans receiving nothing from then-President Bill Clinton. And that government shutdown followed the one in November 1995, when Republicans received merely an agreement from President Clinton to balance the budget within seven years.

Notice a pattern? The president always wins government shutdowns. Congress never does.

Why is that? It's because Americans now buy into the urgency of funding the government fully. We've been trained for years that any government shutdown imperils us all: The zombie apocalypse is coming. The media have aided the cause of a growing government admirably here. This week, CNN ran a segment suggesting that a government shutdown could prevent us from tracking an inbound asteroid that could wipe out all life on Earth. Then we wonder why so many Americans are so deeply disturbed at the possibility of a shutdown that would allow Medicare and Social Security to operate largely unimpeded, that would allow the Veterans Affairs hospitals to remain open and military function to continue (though pay would be backlogged).

We also have been trained for years that the power of the purse is in the hands of the Congress, not the executive. That means we see the Congress as the party most responsible for passing legislation the president will sign, not the president as the party most responsible for agreeing with Congress. And that means that the president's priorities take center stage when dealing with Congress, even though the president is oftentimes the person holding up government funding.

Here, in essence, is the problem: We're addicted to government. The population is addicted to the notion that the government operates without the bumps and breaks uniquely built into the American system; the media are addicted to the daily show of government; the members of government are happy to keep spending cash and scare the life out of constituents when the spending stops.

Make no mistake: The Democrats' strategy and rationale for the government shutdown was awful. But if Americans have been so conditioned to panic regarding such shutdowns that 69 hours—48 of them over a weekend—drive us to fever pitch, we have much bigger problems than a few lost work hours.

A New Kind of Gridlock

March 28, 2018

When the Founding Fathers wrote the Constitution of the United States, they feared the possibility of partisanship overtaking rights-based government. To that end, they crafted a system of checks and balances designed to pit interest against interest, promoting gridlock over radical change. The founders saw legislators, presidents and judges as ambitious in their pursuit of power.

They could not have foreseen our politicians.

Our politicians aren't so much ambitious for power as they are afraid of accountability. And so, we have a new sort of gridlock on Capitol Hill: Politicians campaign in cuttingly partisan fashion and then proceed to avoid solving just the sorts of issues on which they campaigned.

Last week, for example, Republicans passed a massive $1.3 trillion omnibus funding package to avert a government shutdown. It included full funding for Planned Parenthood and the regional Gateway rail project, but not full funding for the border wall. Republicans had spent years decrying deficits, criticizing funding for Planned Parenthood and ripping useless stimulus spending; they'd spent years clamoring for a border wall. When push came to shove, they did nothing.

Meanwhile, Democrats tore into the Republican budget for failing to ensure the permanent residence of so-called DREAMers, immigrants living in the United States illegally who were brought to the country as children. Then they rallied in Washington, D.C., along with gun control-minded students from Parkland, Florida, calling for more regulations on the Second Amendment. When Democrats held control of Congress and the presidency from 2009 to 2011, however, they promulgated no new gun legislation and passed no protection for DREAMers. Instead, then-President Barack Obama issued an executive action during his re-election cycle after saying repeatedly that he could not legally do so, and he complained incessantly about guns.

So, what should this tell us?

It should tell us that we, the voters, are suckers.

Our politicians use hot-button political issues in order to gin up the base and get us out to vote. They talk about how they'll end funding for Planned Parenthood and cut back spending on the right; they talk about how they'll end gun violence and protect DREAMers on the left. Then, once in power, they instead focus on broadly popular legislation instead of passing the legislation they've promised. They campaign for their base, but they govern for the center.

So, what are the *real* differences between the parties? The Republican Party is in favor of tax cuts and defense spending; the Democratic Party is in favor of increased regulation and social spending. All the other discussion points are designed merely to drive passion.

Practically speaking, this means gridlock on the issues about which Americans care most. Don't expect Republicans to stop funding Planned Parenthood anytime soon. And don't expect Democrats to start pushing serious gun control. They keep those issues alive deliberately to inflame excitement during election campaigns. Then, once in power, those issues go back into the freezer, to emerge and be defrosted when the time is right.

It's a convenient ploy. It means that partisan voters will never buck their party—after all, if the other side gets into power, they'll *really* go nuts. And, hey, maybe *this time*, our party bosses won't lie to us.

But they will. And we'll swallow it. And the government will grow. But at least we'll have the comfort slamming one another over issues that will never get solved.

Supreme Court: Be Polite When You Violate Others' Rights

June 6, 2018

This week, the Supreme Court ruled on the Masterpiece Cakeshop case. That case involved a religious Christian man, Jack Phillips, who decorates cakes for a living. Two men came into his shop one day and demanded that Phillips decorate a cake for their same-sex wedding. Phillips refused. For this grave breach of civic duty, the Colorado Civil Rights Commission referred his case for prosecution, ruling that he had breached the customers' rights to receive service.

The Supreme Court ignored the key issues of the case. It refused to countenance whether First Amendment speech rights could be violated in favor of nondiscrimination laws—whether, for example, a gay songwriter could be forced to perform work for an evangelical Christian choir looking for a tune to liven up Leviticus 18. It refused to consider whether First Amendment free association rights could be completely overthrown by reference to nondiscrimination laws— whether any business could be told to serve anyone for any reason at any time. Finally, it refused to consider whether First Amendment freedom of religion could be overturned in favor of nondiscrimination law—whether religious practice stops at the front door of the home and the church.

Instead, the court ruled that the baker didn't have to bake the cake because the members of the Colorado Civil Rights Commission were unduly mean. You see, the commission pilloried the man's religious viewpoint rather than giving it a respectful hearing; it compared his viewpoint to pro-slavery and pro-Holocaust viewpoints. This was extreme and nasty. Thus, Justice Anthony Kennedy concluded: "The commission's hostility was inconsistent with the First Amendment's guarantee that our laws be applied in a manner that is neutral toward religion. ... The outcome of cases like this in other circumstances must await further elaboration in the courts."

I must have missed the "be kind; rewind" section of the First Amendment.

Of course, the Supreme Court likely ruled on narrow grounds in order to achieve a 7-2 majority including liberal Justices Elena Kagan and Stephen Breyer. But the ruling bodes ill for the future: It doesn't protect religious Americans, nor does it protect freedom of speech.

In reality, the founders would have been aghast at this issue ever rising to the level of the judiciary. Freedom of speech, and, by extension, freedom of association, were designed to allow private individuals to live their lives as they see fit, free of the burden of an overreaching government. Freedom of religion was to be guaranteed by a small government unconcerned with the day-to-day matters of business. Free markets were considered enough incentive to prevent mass discrimination in public accommodations.

Now, however, the courts have decided that the government can tell you what to say, who to say it to and how to act out your religion. The only holdup is that they have to be nice about telling you what to do.

When Government Becomes Everything, Everything Becomes Crazy

September 12, 2018

This week, Republican congressional candidate Rudy Peters of California was nearly stabbed by a 35-year-old Castro Valley resident, Farzad Fazeli. According to media reports, Fazeli started shouting about President Trump and then pulled out a switchblade. Thankfully, the switchblade malfunctioned, and Peters was able to fend of Fazeli, who was eventually arrested.

This is far from the only case of political violence we've seen in recent years. The most famous was, of course, the congressional baseball shooting by a crazed Bernie Sanders supporter. House Majority Whip Steve Scalise, R-La., was nearly murdered during the carnage. Now Scalise says: "You've got some people on the left that just want this idea of resist ... you've gotten to where there are death threats and literal attacks on lives ... and frankly, what I want to see is the left stand up against this."

Meanwhile, the right has seen its own violent crazies. Last month, Robert Chain, 68, of California was arrested after allegedly calling The Boston Globe newsroom and threatening to shoot employees. During that call, he called the newspaper the "enemy of the people," echoing the language of President Trump.

So, is the left responsible for Peters? Is President Trump responsible for Chain? Of course not. As always, in a free society, people are responsible for their own actions. Unless a political actor openly calls for violence and that call is heeded, that actor shouldn't be blamed for the violence of acolytes.

With that said, something is deeply wrong.

What's deeply wrong is that we now attribute all failings to the government and all successes to the government. Take, for example, the Washington Post, which suggested in an editorial this week that

President Trump is "complicit" about Hurricane Florence because he doesn't support the Post's preferred climate change policy. Now, whatever your feelings about Trump's climate change policy or lack thereof, he's not responsible for a hurricane any more than Barack Obama was responsible for Hurricane Sandy. At best, Trump's policy *may* be contributing to future global warming. But that's not the Post's suggestion. Instead, the Post editors suggest that Trump is himself a King Triton, stirring the seas into hurricane-friendly territory.

By contrast, those on the right suggest that President Trump is solely responsible for our economic boom. They're not wrong to attribute some of the economic growth to consumer confidence and business investment in the wake of Trump's pro-capitalism policies. But Trump isn't any more "in charge" of the economy than Obama was. The economy is far too complex and government is far too complicated for executive tinkering to be attributed to success or blamed for failure.

But we're addicted to our belief in the primal power of our politicians. Once we believe that Trump is either the Great Satan or the Great God, it's no wonder that fringe actors on either side are willing to take extreme measures to harm or "protect" him. The only solution: We must realize that the president is merely a constitutional officer bound by the checks and balances of his role. And we must stop attributing to politics control over our lives that politics does not truly exert.

When Checks and Balances Fail

January 16, 2019

In February 2017, Dr. Christopher Duntsch became the first surgeon in American history known to be sentenced to prison for botching a patient surgery. A licensed neurosurgeon, Duntsch left a string of deaths and maimed bodies in his wake: He was accused of causing the death of two surgery patients and leaving 33 others permanently damaged. His patients left their lives in his hands; he left them paralyzed or dead.

The checks and balances that were supposed to contain Duntsch failed utterly. His medical school licensed him but didn't require the preparation necessary to instill competence. Hospitals suspended him but didn't report him. The medical board could do nothing without forms filed against him. Patients were left without recourse.

When checks and balances fail, damage is usually the result.

That's why when it came to our system of government, the founders were so focused on creating gridlock. They recognized that in a system in which legitimacy sprang from popular support, the easy path to perdition lay in popularly backed centralized power—tyranny could spring just as easily from a popular majority as from a king or despot. The founders didn't trust individuals with authority, and they didn't trust human beings to delegate authority to mere individuals.

But popular governments have always bucked against such limitations.

The majority of Americans always want action, on some grounds or others. That leads to an eternal drive to grant unchecked power to some institution of government. As Alexis de Tocqueville writes in his 1840 "Democracy in America": "It may easily be foreseen that almost all the able and ambitious members of a democratic community will labor without ceasing to extend the powers of government, because they all hope at some time or other to wield those powers. ... Centralization will be the natural government."

We're now seeing the consequences of such centralization on two separate fronts: the president's authority to declare a national emergency and the FBI's investigations into the president. Proponents of President Trump would like to see power centralized in the presidency; antagonists of President Trump would like to see power centralized in the FBI.

President Trump's allies seem eager for Trump to declare a national emergency in order to appropriate funds for a border wall. The law cuts against such a declaration: The National Emergencies Act was written to curtail presidential authority, not increase it. No matter how much border hawks (including me) want a border barrier, the proper method is to request funds from Congress.

Meanwhile, President Trump's enemies are celebrating reports this week that the FBI investigated Trump as a possible Russian agent after his firing of then-FBI director James Comey. Trump had authority under the Constitution to fire Comey, and there's no actual evidence that Trump is an agent of the Russians. But Trump's enemies want the legislature to step in and attempt to protect the FBI from executive branch checks on it.

All of this is foolish. It's *good* that the legislative branch checks the executive branch, and it's *good* that the executive branch must remain in control of executive branch agencies. Here's the easy test: How would you feel if the situations were reversed? How would Republicans feel about an emergency declaration from a Democratic president to shift funds to leftist priorities? How would Democrats feel about Republican attempts to seize control of the FBI for purposes of investigating a Democratic president?

Nobody ought to trust institutions enough to grant them unchecked power. And no one ought to trust the people enough to allow us to do so.

Government Isn't the Social Fabric

March 13, 2019

Over the weekend, Democratic Fresh Face and socialist darling Rep. Alexandria Ocasio-Cortez, D-N.Y., spoke at the South by Southwest conference. While sitting amidst the enormous bounty provided by capitalism—top-notch electronic equipment, a massive crowd of paid ticket holders—AOC tore into capitalism. She called the system that has raised 80 percent of the globe from extreme poverty since 1980 "irredeemable." She railed against the injustice of people having to work jobs rather than write poetry—as though socialist countries are famous for ensuring that people work only the jobs they find spiritually rewarding.

Finally, she settled on her most damning line of attack: America as it currently stands is "garbage," because in the United States, "if you don't have a job, you are left to die."

That's an odd critique given the long history of death associated with socialism—some 45 million deaths under Mao, some 30 to 40 million under Stalin and some 2 million under Pol Pot, for starters. But it's an even odder critique given the fact that life expectancy has radically increased under capitalism: In 1850, the average European life expectancy was 36.3 years, while today, the average life expectancy across Europe stands at approximately 80. Furthermore, the United States currently boasts effective full employment. Our poor are in danger of dying of *obesity*, not starvation. And we spend, on a state and federal level, at least $1.1 trillion per year on means-tested welfare programs. By census data, that amounts to nearly $9,000 per household in the United States annually, or nearly $28,000 for every person living in poverty in the United States.

But let's take Ocasio-Cortez's argument to the logical extreme. Presumably, she's in favor of these expensive government programs and thinks that in their absence, the poor would be left to die in the United States. Is that true?

Absolutely not. Ocasio-Cortez makes the same mistake so many on the left do: She conflates government redistributionism with the social fabric itself. In her view, there is no social fabric absent government. What's more, nongovernmental social fabric is a *threat* to equality—as Sen. Bernie Sanders, I-Vt., put it in 1981, "I don't believe in charities." The New York Times reported that Sanders questioned the "fundamental concepts on which charities are based," since government was the only entity positioned to help the impoverished.

That's sheer nonsense. Before the rise of the massive welfare state, Americans gave massive amounts of charity. In 1926, religious congregations spent more than $150 million on projects other than church maintenance and upkeep, with state governments spending just $23 million and local governments spending $37 million, according to economists Jonathan Gruber of MIT and Daniel Hungerman of the University of Notre Dame. Americans have always given enormous sums to charity. And those charitable activities come along with something government redistributionism can't achieve: a feeling of social belonging and of membership in a social fabric.

Free markets create prosperity. And government isn't the social fabric. Recognition of those two simple facts explains what made America thrive—and can help us thrive again, in spite of those who would prefer to tear down markets and social fabric and replace them with the heavy hand of centralized government.

Why the Left Is Reconsidering Al Franken

July 24, 2019

On Monday, The New Yorker printed a lengthy piece by reporter Jane Mayer about the sad fate of former Sen. Al Franken, D-Minn. Franken resigned from the Senate in 2017 after a bevy of women accused him of sexual harassment; their accounts ranged from unwanted kisses to unsolicited a-- grabbing. In the midst of the #MeToo movement, Franken stepped down, all the while decrying President Trump's own record of allegations concerning mistreatment of women.

At the time, there were two possible interpretations of events. The first was more inspiring: After decades of defending sexual misconduct by powerful Democratic figures, Democrats and their media allies were finally willing to reset a social standard. In the wake of #MeToo, they had reconsidered their worship of Teddy Kennedy, their pathetic willingness to cover for Bill Clinton. A new day had dawned.

Then there was the second, more cynical theory: Democrats and their media allies were looking to set a new standard out of pure partisanship. They weren't really concerned about Franken's victims any more than they had been about Clinton's victims. Instead, they were looking to establish a level of morally superior ground upon which to attack Trump and demand that Republicans disown him.

This week, we found out which theory was true.

Mayer, the New Yorker reporter, rose to public acclaim just last year when she reported on then-Supreme Court nominee Brett Kavanaugh's supposed sexual evils. With no supporting facts other than the hazy accounts of decades-old events, she attacked Kavanaugh with alacrity. Now, however, she has flipped: She's concerned with Franken's lack of due process; she questions the political motivations of one of his accusers; she points out that the evidence is supposedly scanty. Democrats, too, have risen to Franken's defense. Many now claim that Sen. Kirsten Gillibrand, D-N.Y., was the real villain in this scenario, having rushed for Franken's scalp precipitously.

In other words, Franken was kicked out of the party when Democrats were trying to build a case against Trump. Now that they've concluded that case won't work, they want Franken back again. Presumably, they'll soon be back to praising Clinton, too.

This sort of behavior is deeply destructive to American public discourse. That's because a standard upheld *only* as a weapon to target political opposition is no standard at all. What's more, the partisan interpretation of the standard creates an incentive for opponents to violate their own commitment to the standard. It's a classic prisoner's dilemma: The person who actually abides by a common moral standard and speaks out against bad behavior on all sides ends up the sucker. Only a fool would call out his own side to the cheers of opponents while his opponents defend their own degencrates.

The problem of politically motivated standards isn't restricted to sexual abuse. It extends to race: Why should Republicans condemn President Trump's tweets about the so-called Squad while Democrats maintain support for Rep. Ilhan Omar's anti-Semitism and Rep. Ayanna Pressley's racism? Why should Republicans provide ammunition to their ill-motivated opponents?

The only way to restore a common standard in politics is for both sides to rebuild trust, step by step. And *that* can only happen when both sides share common goals and values. Otherwise, everyone will decide that losing by abiding by the rules must take a back seat to victory by any means. And that means the destruction of our standards, one by one, until there are no standards left.

We're getting pretty close already.

The Economy: Capitalism & Freedom

History suggests that capitalism is a necessary condition for political freedom. Clearly it is not a sufficient condition.
—Milton Friedman

Why the Image of the Great Economic Leader Is Dangerous

January 12, 2017

On Tuesday, Alibaba CEO Jack Ma, one of the richest men on the planet, met with President-elect Donald Trump at Trump Tower. After emerging from the meeting, he stood alongside Trump and announced: "We specifically talked about ... supporting 1 million small businesses, especially in the Midwest of America. Small businesses on the platform selling products—agriculture products and American services—to China and Asia because we're pretty big in Asia." Trump shook Ma's hand in front of the cameras and announced, "Jack and I are going to do some great things," before shaking hands.

This is good news, obviously. Bringing investment to the United States is worthwhile, and opening trade is excellent. The minipresser was skimpy on details, as most of Trump's economic big-win meetings have been. What does Ma get in return for the headline? Or is he simply moving toward investment in the United States on the basis of broad-based economic policy, including deregulation, from Trump?

There is one big problem with photo ops like this: They promote the myth that great men run the economy.

Since Trump's election, he has met at Trump Tower with CEOs from major companies and then trotted them out to the press, shaken their hands and announced new investments. This is in Trump's interest—he gets terrific headlines about how his very presence has boosted the economy. It's in the interest of the individual companies, too—they are on the good graces of the president-elect, plus they get the halo effect of being perceived as more patriotic and self-sacrificing.

But this routine creates the impression that the economy is essentially a series of negotiations between the president of the United States and individual companies, that the economy is, in simple terms, a rigged game. Advocates for such optics thrill to them. Isn't it showing that Trump is business-friendly? Doesn't it demonstrate that an activist commander in chief can bring the economy roaring back so long as he exerts the force of his will?

It's the force-of-will argument that's troubling to advocates of economic freedom. Economies do not thrive because command-and-control businessmen determine the fortunes of individual companies, or because they threaten individual businesses with governmental repercussions if they dare to engage in profit-maximizing activities. Economies thrive because of broad, consistent policies that create reward for positive risk-taking and increased productivity.

But the aesthetic of the Great Leader standing beside the Great Businessman runs precisely contrary to this reality. It fulfills a public thirst for someone to run things, even though that thirst generates an outsized picture of what the president can and should do. The aesthetic perpetuates an ugly cycle: Great Leader purportedly runs the economy in coordination with business; economy goes south; Great Leader blames business; public calls for more power for Great Leader; and businesses are called onto the carpet to make concessions to the Great Leader. All of this generates a less free, less dynamic economy.

We can all cheer news that more companies want to invest in the United States; we can all hope and pray that Donald Trump's economic policy draws more dollars and jobs to the country. But we should *not* fall prey to the economic misconception that the president ought to act as a benevolent economic dictator, bestowing favor upon all those who please him.

But Reality Isn't Fair

June 28, 2017

In 2014, I debated Seattle City Council member and avowed socialist Kshama Sawant. Sawant was one of the chief proponents of a city ordinance that would create a $15 minimum wage. Eventually, the city adopted a three-phase transition plan that would push minimum wage to $11 per hour, then $13 per hour, then $15 per hour. In our debate, I asked Sawant directly whether she would support a $1,000 minimum wage. She deflected the question, of course. She deflected the question because reality would not allow for a $1,000 minimum wage. Were the government to mandate such an idiocy, every business in the Seattle area would immediately cut back employment, and all of those seeking minimum wage jobs would end up losing their income.

As it turns out, it didn't take a $1,000 minimum wage to destroy the income for minimum wage workers. Thirteen dollars was plenty. According to a paper from The National Bureau of Economic Research, "the minimum wage ordinance lowered low-wage employees' earnings by an average of $125 per months in 2016."

All of this was foreseeable, given the fact that businesses compete with one another to lower cost and thus operate with slim profit margins. That means businesses have two choices when government forcibly raises labor costs: increase prices and thereby lower demand, or cut back on the work force. Businesses opted to do the latter in order to stay competitive.

Reality is unpleasant. Perhaps that's why so few politicians seem willing to face up to it.

On a larger scale, the bipartisan consensus in favor of regulations that force insurance companies to cover pre-existing conditions mirrors the minimum wage debate. It is perfectly obvious that forcing insurance companies—professional risk assessors that determine pricing based on actuarial estimates as to health—to cover those with pre-existing conditions costs them an enormous amount of money. If you are a consumer, why would you bother buying a health insurance plan while healthy, when you could wait to do so until after your costs materialize? Yet both parties would rather cater to the foolish notion that it is "unfair" for insurance companies to act as insurance companies than allow insurance companies to do what they do best: create a market to allow Americans to exercise choice.

But in economics, once one heresy has been advanced, a slew of other heresies follow. Coverage of pre-existing conditions has to be subsidized somehow. Democrats propose to mandate that people buy health insurance; this violates freedom of choice and artificially increases premiums for the healthy in order to pay for the sick. Republicans propose subsidies to encourage purchase, artificially creating demand without allowing the competition among health plans that would keep premiums down.

But everyone is surprised when such schemes fail.

They shouldn't be. Politics used to be the art of educating the public about reality and pushing for change where change is possible. Now politics is the art of convincing the public that you can make reality disappear if it votes for you. Sadly, our politicians can't make reality disappear. And every time they try to do so, reality comes rushing back with a vengeance.

Google's Leftist Goggles Leave Googlers Agog

August 9, 2017

So, Google is a leftist company.

That's no surprise. All you'd have to do to verify that fact is watch the rotating Google doodles throughout the year. They frequently feature social justice warriors, leftist causes celebres and random slaps at religion. Or you could check its search results, which tend to favor leftist causes and politicians over conservative ones.

But Google isn't just liberal; it's leftist. It's so leftist that its vice president of Diversity, Integrity & Governance, Danielle Brown, participated in a public scourging of an unnamed Google employee who had the temerity to question the company's odd focus on "diversity" hires. The employee penned a 10-page Jerry Maguire-style memo outlining Google's obsession with "diversity" and why its practices amount to illegal discrimination—and pointing out that the lack of women in top positions reflects scientific differences between men and women on average, not discriminatory social policy.

This intrepid soul openly signaled his opposition to sexism but then pointed out that personality differences between men and women on average, as well as men's higher drive for status, could lead to wage gaps at the company. That is absolutely correct based on a tremendous amount of available social science data. In fact, it's also true that while women on average may slightly outperform men on IQ tests, more men are found at the extremes of the bell curve— there are more men on the upper and lower ends of the spectrum. That would lead to the hiring of more men at prestigious companies like Google based on merit, not based on sexism.

But according to Google itself, such wrongthink must be curbed. And so, Brown stated that the memo "advanced incorrect assumptions about gender." Not controversial—incorrect. The facts, you see, must be made to fit Google's theory. Furthermore, said Brown, "I'm not going to link to it here as it's not a viewpoint that I or this company endorses." But there was good news. "Diversity and inclusion are a fundamental part of our values and the culture we continue to cultivate," she said.

Yay, diversity! Shut up, guy who disagrees!

Unfortunately, this philosophy of diversity before freedom or merit has run amok at many of America's major companies. And it has an impact on product. YouTube has reportedly been restricting videos it deems controversial or inappropriate, and disproportionately targeting comics like Steven Crowder and educators like Dennis Prager. Facebook has taken steps in recent months to curb its own biases, but only after a blowup with conservatives who were angry at its apparent attempts to crack down on non-leftists. Twitter has banned or suspended conservatives for mysterious reasons that it has never applied to members of the left.

Google has a pair of leftist goggles on at all times. Its users shouldn't have blinders on about it. Every search result should be scanned for algorithmic bias. After all, a company that will rip its own employee to shreds for defending its hiring practices on the basis of science and data will do anything to defend its leftist politics.

Democrats' Newest Plan: Nationalized Health Care

September 13, 2017

On Monday, two seemingly unrelated headlines made the news. The first: America's national debt had finally reached $20 trillion. The second: New Jersey Democratic Sen. Cory Booker had finally come out in favor of Vermont independent Sen. Bernie Sanders' magical, mythical "Medicare-For-All" plan.

Of course, the two aren't unrelated at all. Once again, the Democratic Party is signing checks the country can't cash. Sanders' Medicare-For-All scheme would add some $13.8 trillion in spending over the first decade alone. Medicare already carries $58 trillion in unfunded liabilities, according to National Review. How unrealistic is Medicare-For-All? It's so unrealistic that the state of California has rejected a single-payer health care for being too expensive—and California currently has a Democratic supermajority in the state assembly.

Yet Democrats continue to push further and further to the left, fearful of being outflanked. Booker isn't alone in his newfound embrace of socialized medicine. California's Sen. Kamala Harris has also endorsed Sanders' ridiculous plan. Massachusetts Sen. Elizabeth Warren will be co-sponsoring Sanders' plan, as will Democratic Sen. Jeff Merkley of Oregon.

Why? Because Democrats are deeply frightened of being outflanked by socialists. There's no benefit to moving to the center when your base sees no purpose in fiscal responsibility. So instead, Democrats race one another to the Soviet Union.

Meanwhile, Republicans cower in fear. Afraid of making the case for freedom, they compete with Democrats to see who can administer the giant state more "efficiently," as though efficiency were the key problem with statism. Thus, Republicans ran headlong from the possibility of repealing Obamacare, afraid that the American people would backlash against them for "taking away" some form of entitlement.

This is a mistake by Republicans. Yes, whoever touches entitlements pays a price. But that's not true if the alternative is a slide into total governmental control. That's the case Republicans made from the day Obamacare was initiated: that it was the first step toward socialized medicine. Now Democrats are showing that the Republican critique was true. Republicans ought to provide a binary choice here: Either slide into nationalized health care with Democrats or help us tear away the bulwarks of tyranny in health care in favor of freedom.

In exposing their own radicalism, the Democrats have provided Republicans with an opportunity to seize the middle with conservatism. Republicans need not bend before the media's insistence that health care is a government responsibility—they can easily and honestly point at the Democratic frontrunners and identify the agenda. The question is whether Republicans have the courage to do so or whether they've bought the false narrative that President Trump won because he campaigned as a centrist. Trump won promising full Obamacare repeal. Republicans can do the same now and have the credibility of an awful alternative behind them.

All it takes is courage. Democratic cowardice has led the Party down the primrose path to full-on socialism. Now, Republicans must either make a stand against it or be complicit in bringing about that regime.

Fiscal Responsibility or Lower Taxes?

December 6, 2017

This week, Republicans in the Senate finally passed their long-awaited tax reform plan. It lowers individual income tax rates across the board, although it does claw back some government revenue in the form of elimination of state and local tax deductions. It drops corporate tax rates as well. It is, in other words, a significant but not atypical Republican tax cut designed to boost economic growth by allowing Americans to keep more of their own money.

The tax cut will almost certainly increase the deficit, however. Even with dynamic scoring—the assumption that the economy will grow at a faster clip thanks to tax cuts—the tax cuts could lead to $1 trillion in lower revenue through 2027. This has led some conservatives to sour on tax reform altogether, rightly saying that Republicans were, until a few months ago, complaining incessantly about former President Obama's blowout deficits and the burgeoning national debt, which now stands at a cool $20.5 trillion. That doesn't include long-term unfunded liabilities, which are slated to bring the debt to some $70 to 75 trillion in coming decades.

So, which is more important: cutting deficits or cutting taxes?

The answer, in the long run, is obvious: cutting deficits. Deficits impoverish future generations; they undermine the credibility of our financial commitments; they prevent us from fulfilling promises we have already made to our own citizens. There are already millions of Americans who will never receive Social Security in the amount they have been promised; there are already millions of Americans unborn who will spend their lives paying off the commitments made by others for political gain.

At the same time, were we to raise taxes to pay off our debts, we would enervate our population and inure citizens to high taxes. Citizens of European states are used to insanely high tax rates; the impetus for spending cuts based on desire for lower taxes disappears after years of habituation to those tax rates and unsustainable government benefits. Europeans are used to the very social programs that continue to bankrupt them despite high tax rates; they're not clamoring to cut programs based on their distaste for those tax rates.

This puts American politicians in somewhat of a Catch-22. If they stump for spending cuts, they're cast as uncaring and cruel; if they stump for tax increases to pay for those spending cuts, they're cast as uncaring and cruel. Thus, the deficit continues to grow.

So, what should Republicans do about it? They ought to cut taxes, and then they ought to acknowledge that cuts are necessary to keep taxes low. Let Americans get used to keeping their own money. Let them understand that services aren't free. Then, be honest about the costs associated with big government programs.

In the end, both Democrats and Republicans will have to face a simple truth: It's either government cuts or bust. There's no reason for Republicans to give away their only leverage—the taste of the public for a dynamic economy based on individuals retaining their earnings—in order to shore up programs Democrats will only work to expand.

What the Courts Are for

July 4, 2018

Democrats are in a state of sheer panic.

They're panicking because last week, Justice Anthony Kennedy—a reliable vote in favor of certain leftist priorities including abortion and same-sex marriage—announced that he will step down from the Supreme Court, leaving President Trump a second selection. This apparently will lead to the end of a free America. According to Jeffrey Toobin of CNN, the remade Supreme Court will spell doom: "Abortion illegal; doctors prosecuted; gay people barred from restaurants, hotels, stores; African-Americans out of elite schools; gun control banned in 50 states; the end of regulatory state."

None of this is true, of course. It simply demonstrates the wild overreach to which the left has subjected the judicial branch to date.

The judicial branch was never meant to act as a superlegislature, using the verbiage of the Constitution in order to implement preferred policy prescriptions. In Federalist No. 78, Alexander Hamilton expressed the idea well: "The courts must declare the sense of the law; and if they should be disposed to exercise WILL instead of JUDGMENT, the consequence would equally be the substitution of their pleasure to that of the legislative body." Substituting will for judgment would make the case for utterly dissolving the judicial branch.

Yet according to the Democrats, the Supreme Court *should* exercise will instead of judgment. The role of the court, according to Justice Sonia Sotomayor, is to help expedite change in our society: "Our society would be strait-jacketed were not the courts, with the able assistance of the lawyers, constantly overhauling the law and adapting it to the realities of ever-changing social, industrial and political conditions." Justice Elena Kagan believes the same thing, which is why she constantly describes the Constitution as "abstract," leaving her room to interpret it as poetry rather than statute.

This is why Democrats celebrate obviously superlegal decisions like Roe v. Wade: There is no right to abortion in the Constitution, but they would prefer not to battle that issue out at the electoral level. The Supreme Court allows them to hand down their policy from the mountaintop without having to subject those policies to public scrutiny.

And *that* means that any reversal of such policy by a Supreme Court that actually reads the Constitution as it was written is a threat to Democratic hegemony. Were President Trump to appoint an originalist to the Supreme Court, Roe v. Wade would surely die, but that wouldn't make abortion illegal—the issue would have to be put before the American public. Affirmative action from state schools would end, but African-Americans wouldn't be barred from attending elite institutions—such a bar would remain illegal. Gays across the country would not suddenly find themselves barred from public restaurants—it's unlikely the Supreme Court would rule such action legal, and even if it were to do so, virtually no establishments across the country would start asking about sexual orientation at the door.

In the end, the Democrats' obsession with the Supreme Court says more about them than about the role of the court. It says that they don't believe their policies are popular enough to win the country over at the electoral level. If the judiciary should be returned to its role of ruling by judgment rather than will, the will of the people might be heard once again—and it wouldn't be friendly to Democrats. Democrats know it. Hence the panic.

Being a Socialist Means Never Having to Say You're Sorry

August 9, 2018

"So, how are you planning to pay for that?"

This should be the first question asked about any political program. Unfortunately, it's not. And that's why Sen. Bernie Sanders, I-Vt., and congressional candidate Alexandria Ocasio-Cortez, D-N.Y., are thought leaders for their parties.

Take Sanders. He has been promoting his "Medicare for All" slogan for years. The left loves it. Among the top Democrats who have embraced this slogan are Sen. Cory Booker, D-N.J., Sen. Elizabeth Warren, D-Mass., Sen. Kamala Harris, D-Calif., and Sen. Jeff Merkley, D-Ore. Most of those senators want to run for president. So they understand that Sanders' bumper sticker policy is popular on its face.

There's only one problem: Nobody asked that first question. This week, Charles Blahous of the Mercatus Center at George Mason University released a study taking a look at the cost of Sanders' preferred program. The total: $32.6 trillion over 10 years. Over that same period, our *total* federal spending is projected at $56 trillion—and we're already racking up debt like there's no tomorrow on that budget. That means that we could double our taxes at every level and still not come close to covering Sanders' program.

Sanders responded to this unfortunate news by attacking the study, blaming the nefarious Koch brothers for sponsoring Blahous' basic math. There's only one problem: The Urban Institute, a left-leaning outlet, estimated the cost at $32 trillion. So this isn't a right-left problem. It's a basic math problem. Sanders doesn't understand basic math.

Or, more accurately, he doesn't care about it. And he's not alone. Ocasio-Cortez recently embarrassed herself on this same topic.

When asked about how she would pay for her program of free Medicare for All, college tuition and housing, she explained that we could just raise the corporate tax rate to 28% and close some loopholes, and "that's $2 trillion right there." Which would pay for ... approximately seven months of Medicare for All. Then, Ocasio-Cortez explained that she'd find money by cutting the defense budget ($700 billion per year), which would *still* not cover Medicare for All. And she'd create a carbon tax, which could crush industry, leading to lesser tax revenue.

But Democrats aren't interested in who pays for things, because their ultimate solution is that *nobody pays for things*. Yes, really. According to Stephanie Kelton, professor of public policy and economics at Stony Brook University—and a Sanders 2016 advisor—we can simply pay for things by paying for things. She says the only limit on spending is inflation. Even Paul Krugman of The New York Times has called this idea foolhardy: Inflation is inevitable once people realize that the government is literally just printing money to spend it, and once people begin socking away cash in order to avoid the exorbitant taxes they're sure will come.

The good news for Democrats is that nobody asks the key question. Even Republicans don't, which is why they spend trillions of dollars of their own. And so long as nobody is asking the question, Sanders and Ocasio-Cortez will be the future of the country ... until we run out of money.

The Ungrateful Nation

November 21, 2018

Here are a few facts about America.

The unemployment rate among those with a high school education is 3.9%. The poorest quintile of Americans have seen their post-tax incomes increase 80% since 1979, according to Congressional Budget Office data, and post-tax and transfer income for that quintile has skyrocketed 32% since 2000. The upper-middle class in America constituted 13% of the population in 1979; as of 2014, it constituted 30%. According to Pew Research from 2015, when it comes to standard of living, "The U.S. stands head and shoulders above the rest of the world. More than half (56%) of Americans were high income by the global standard ... and 2% were poor."

Fantastic products are cheaper than ever. Human Progress investigated the amount of time Americans must spend to earn enough money to buy key products and found that since 1979, the amount of time spent to earn a refrigerator had dropped 52%, 95% for microwaves, 65% for gas ranges and 61% for dishwashers. Between the mid-1960s and 2007, Americans were able to work less and leisure more: They worked nearly eight hours fewer per week, according to The Heritage Foundation. The wage gap is almost entirely a myth: Women who work the same jobs as men for the same number of hours, and have the same work history and same education as men make the same as men. The chief obstacles to income mobility in the United States are related to personal decision-making, not racial discrimination: As the Brookings Institution points out, of the people who finish high school, get a full-time job and wait until age 21 to get married and have children, nearly 75% join the middle class, and just 2% remain in poverty.

What of freedom? In America, people of all religions practice freely, so long as the government isn't attempting to cram social justice down on them. People are free to speak, so long as government actors aren't utilizing the heckler's veto. We are free to use the press, free to associate and free to protest.

All of this is the result of the greatest governmental philosophy ever committed to paper: God-given individual rights protected by limited government. We haven't always lived up to that philosophy—in some areas, we've progressed mightily, and in others, we've regressed. But the overall success of the United States should be ringing proof that at the very least, we should be grateful and proud to live here.

Yet as of July 2018, fewer than half of Americans surveyed by Gallup said they are extremely proud to be American. Just 32% of Democrats, down from 56% in 2013, said they are extremely proud to be American; only 42% of independents said are were extremely proud to be American. That's ridiculous. Regardless of political affiliation, we should be proud to live in a society founded on eternal truths, in which we have the ability to thrive based on our own choices.

In 1789, as America struggled to find her footing after a revolution against the most powerful military and economic engine in the world, then-President George Washington issued a proclamation. He thanked God for "his kind care and protection of the People of this Country," for "the great degree of tranquility, union, and plenty, which we have since enjoyed—for the peaceable and rational manner, in which we have been enabled to establish constitutions of government for our safety and happiness."

If Washington could urge gratefulness in 1789, we'd be fools not to do so now, when our lives are so much better in every material way. This Thanksgiving, let's remember what we have—and let's remember the eternal ideas that provide the groundwork for our prosperity.

'Medicare-for-All' Is No Health Care Cure-All

November 28, 2018

This week, congresswoman-elect Alexandria Ocasio-Cortez, D-N.Y., tweeted out a letter from Spectrum Health to one Hedda Elizabeth Martin. The letter described the clinic's rejection of a heart transplant for Martin based on lack of a "more secure financial plan for immunosuppressive medication coverage." The clinic added, "The Committee is recommending a fundraising effort of $10,000." Ocasio-Cortez tweeted, "Insurance groups are recommending GoFundMe as official policy—where customers can die if they can't raise the goal in time—but sure, single payer healthcare is unreasonable."

First off, Ocasio-Cortez is simply incorrect. The letter itself isn't directly from the insurance company but from the clinic. It declined to perform the heart surgery because the patient didn't have the ability to pay for the medications necessary to prevent organ rejection by the immune system. Furthermore, deductibles on insurance that would cover such drugs under Obamacare would certainly surpass the $10,000 requested by the clinic.

Most of all, though, Martin's health care was provided, in this case, by Medicare Part B. She herself explained via a since-deleted post on Facebook: "with my 20% copay for pharmaceuticals under Part B ... it will cost me about $700 a month for my part B copay for anti-rejection drugs. Once I reach my $4500 annual my cost is $0. So they want me to show I can cover my $4500 deductible by saving $10,000 ... which I will do."

So, would "Medicare-for-all"—Ocasio-Cortez's preferred solution—actually take care of the problem? Or would it exacerbate it, given that nationalized health care creates *more* rationing, not less? There's a reason nationalized health care systems like Sweden's and Britain's have necessitated increased private spending *outside* of the rationed systems. As Scott Atlas of the Hoover

Institution points out: "Sweden has increased its spending on private care for the elderly by 50% in the past decade, abolished its government's monopoly over pharmacies, and made other reforms. Last year alone, the British government spent more than $1 billion on care from private and other non-NHS providers."

And the entire global medical industry benefits from America's private health care spending, which drives the creation of new drugs. So what happens when America no longer covers the cost for such pharmaceuticals? Our Food and Drug Administration may be slow, but it's a lot faster than its European equivalents, which is why the vast majority of new cancer drugs are developed and made available faster in the United States.

In the end, Martin did go to GoFundMe to raise $20,000, not the requisite $10,000. In less than two days, she raised nearly $30,000 from over 400 people. GoFundMe may not be scalable for everyone—but neither is "Medicare-for-all," which is why California scrapped the proposed state version for fear of doubling the budget. Better access to high-quality health care can only be made a reality by an increase in supply, not demand; through innovation, not regulation; through incentivization, not cramdowns. And that means that all of the fulminating over "Medicare-for-all" misses the point and often hangs those most in need out to dry.

Policies Have Consequences

December 5, 2018

This week, France set itself on fire; the stock market tumbled; and news broke that low-wage employment tumbled in the city of Seattle. What do these three headlines have in common? That policies aren't wish lists—they have real-world consequences.

Begin in France, where the so-called "yellow vests"—a group of anti-tax protesters dressed in safety vests—tore up Paris. Rioters defaced the Arc de Triomphe, burned cars and attacked police with stones. They were protesting the exorbitant fuel taxes pursued by French President Emmanuel Macron, taxes designed to curb climate change. The fuel tax rates in France are already estimated to be a whopping 64% on unleaded fuel and 59% on diesel fuel. The riots resulted in the French government backing down, with French Prime Minister Edouard Philippe announcing, "No tax is worth putting in danger the unity of the nation." By polling data, more than 70% of French voters support the yellow vests, and Macron's approval rating has dropped to an anemic 23%.

Move to the United States, where the stock market continued to experience outsized volatility this week—volatility increased by the hot-and-cold pronouncements of President Trump on trade. On Monday, thanks in part to optimistic pronouncements on the postponement of a trade war with China, the Dow Jones Industrial Average rose more than 250 points. On Tuesday, President Trump tweeted that he favors protectionism, dubbing himself "a Tariff Man," and the stock market promptly plummeted more than 600 points. It turns out that talking up the economic benefits of domestic taxation of consumers doesn't do much for consumer confidence or investor optimism.

Now take a look at Seattle, where a new analysis from economists at the University of Washington shows that the city's forced $15 minimum wage had resulted in serious consequences for low-wage workers. The study found that the costs to low-wage workers outpaced benefits "by a ratio of three to one," according to the Washington Post, amounting to an average of $125 per month lost to the average low-wage worker.

But no matter: So long as there are politicians, there will be policies that achieve the opposite of their intended consequences. Politicians, after all, don't have to show results. All they have to demonstrate is a willingness to "help." Thus, the G-20 last year announced that carbon taxes would offer "significant opportunities for modernizing our economies"—workers be damned. President Trump has declared that tariffs are an economic winner, despite reams of evidence to the contrary. And Rep.-elect Alexandria Ocasio-Cortez proclaims that we mustn't "whine about minimum wage"—if we don't implement a minimum wage, we will only be paying "human labor less than they require to live."

Policies have real-world consequences, regardless of how much we wish they don't. It's failure to cope with that basic fact that leads to so much of the finger-pointing we see in politics, with each side accusing the other of bad intention—as though pointing out a policy's failure is equivalent to rooting for failure. It isn't. But rooting for reality is a far more sustainable economic strategy than fighting against it.

Media Runs Rampant

A lie gets halfway around the world before the truth has a chance to get his pants on.
—Winston Churchill

Republicans vs. The Media

November 4, 2015

For years, I have been begging Republicans to stand up to the mainstream media. The left has dominated the media for as long as I've been alive. Yet Republicans have consistently granted leftists in media the patina of legitimacy: they've appeared on their programs, answered their questions without quibble, and allowed the audience to believe that the questions themselves spring from a place of objectivity rather than a desire to harm Republicans.

The political damage has been near incalculable. In 2012, Clinton and George Stephanopoulos singlehandedly redirected the presidential election narrative by asking Republican frontrunner Mitt Romney about banning contraceptives—a policy that no Republican had advocated at any point during the campaign. A few months later, CNN's in-house Barack Obama serviceperson Candy Crowley won the second presidential debate by wrongly telling Romney that Obama had labeled Benghazi a terrorist attack.

So why haven't Republicans fought back? Because Republicans have had a collective action problem. For each Republican willing to label George Stephanopoulos a political hack, there's a camera-loving John McCain willing to grant Stephanopoulos the premise of neutrality for a bit of airtime. For every Republican willing to ask CNBC moderators about their history of leftist questioning, there's a John Kasich willing to praise the moderators as open-minded and fair.

All this came to an end last week. CNBC, in its gauche attempt to grab ratings, set up a rogue's gallery of leftists, all of whom proceeded to berate, bash, and browbeat the various candidates into looking foolish. That continued until Senator Ted Cruz, R., Texas, put a stop to it: "This is not a cage match ... how about talking about the substantive issues people care about?" Cruz pointed out, correctly, that none of the questioners would be voting in a Republican primary—the implication being that the moderators have priorities other than asking honest questions. That started the pile-on. Senator Marco Rubio, R., Fla., jumped in and called the media Hillary Clinton's Super PAC. Governor Chris Christie, R., N.J., bashed moderator John Harwood for being rude, even by New Jersey standards.

And then the candidates came together and said they would no longer abide by rules set by a ratings-seeking, leftist media, and the ratings-seeking, donation-machine Republican National Committee. Instead, they would approve moderators in advance, and demand that those asking the questions be held up to a standard of decency.

The media, naturally, went nearly insane over this slight. Like pearl-clutching CNBC moderator Carl Quintanilla, who peckishly refused to let Cruz answer his question on Obamacare after Cruz slapped the media, the members of the media insisted that the real offenders were the intransigent Republicans. Then the Democratic National Committee announced that MSNBC host Rachel Maddow would be moderating a live presidential forum, humiliating that argument.

The Republican willingness to partake in its own political demise has undermined conservatism for years. Now the mask is off. Thanks to CNBC for that.

The Smug Blind Left Is Trump's Best Friend

May 3, 2017

On Saturday night, Samantha Bee hosted the much-ballyhooed "Not The White House Correspondents' Dinner." The dinner was retitled, of course, because President Trump wasn't enough of a rube to subject himself to three hours of barbs and put-downs by leftists who didn't vote for him and see him as a joke and disdain his voters.

At the dinner, Bee trotted out in a white pantsuit, looking like Kristin Chenoweth playing Hillary Clinton in an alternate-reality version of the 2016 election. "Your job has never been harder," she gushed to the assembled members of the self-pleasing press. "You expose injustice against the weak, and you continue to fact-check the president as if he might someday get embarrassed. Tonight is for you."

Shortly after this ode to the bravery of journalists who maintained silence for eight years of President Barack Obama's lies on Iran and health care, and his Department of Justice targeting the Associated Press and Fox News, Bee appeared on CNN with Jake Tapper. There, she explained of her nearly unwatchable mess of a show, "Full Frontal": "I do the show for me and for people like me, and I don't care how the rest of the world sees it, quite frankly. ... We birth it, and then the world receives it however they want to receive it." During the entirety of this statement, a smug grin was plastered across her face.

Here's a basic rule of thumb: In order to be smug, you generally have to be unaware of your smugness. Bee fits the bill. So do the members of the White House press corps. There is plenty to question about President Trump's administration, from his shifting promises to his knee-jerk reversals, from his policy vagaries to his staffing chaos. But instead of approaching the American people as potential friends to be convinced, smug leftists treat them as ignoramuses.

There's no sincerity involved. Every critique of Trump supporters lumps them all together, and then treats them as gum stuck to the bottom of the shoe of the republic.

Samantha Bee and company have the unmistakable air of the bullies from every high school and college comedy: preening self-obsessed rich kids who sneer at the "losers" who inhabit the hallways, and plan pool parties and taunt the poor kids who can't afford anything better than a beat-up Pinto. The journalist/Hollywood clique is Greg Marmalard from "Animal House," Rod from "Breaking Away" and Regina George from "Mean Girls." They're smug. They're liberal. And that's what drives Trump support.

Trump knows this. That's why he skipped the correspondents dinner and instead went to Pennsylvania, where he held a rally and hilariously declared, "A large group of Hollywood actors and Washington media are consoling each other in a hotel ballroom in our nation's capital right now." It was the best moment for Trump since his speech to a joint session of Congress.

Trump may not be popular among the cool kids. But he's cool enough among them to win supporters in the swing states. If the cool kids don't cut it out, they'll get eight years to mock him and be smug in their assurance that they know what the American people want better than they do.

Trump Didn't Ruin the Media. Obama Did

June 14, 2017

There is a widespread perception among those on the right that President Trump's myriad foibles, vagaries and outright prevarications are somehow justifiable because he is The Great Destroyer of the mainstream media. His fans say he is running the media around in circles—and that is its own reward. Are you still waiting for extreme vetting? For the border wall? For tax cuts, Obamacare repeal and a massive military buildup? Well, sit down and shut up. Just be grateful that Trump has the media hysterically following his tweets like a hormonal teenage boy frantically searching for internet pornography.

But this is wrong.

Trump isn't destroying the media's credibility. They already destroyed their own credibility, thanks to their allegiance to President Barack Obama.

Trump has the benefit of occupying the presidency after Obama. The media was highly critical of President Bill Clinton—even they couldn't ignore the juicy scandals dripping daily from the White House in the 1990s. They were even more critical of President George W. Bush—they were more than willing to misreport in order to undermine a war and destroy a presidency.

But then came Obama.

Obama was the first indicator that the media would simply refuse to cover stories they didn't like about a politician they did. The media covered Clinton's Chinagate and Travelgate. But they refused to cover the IRS scandal with the same level of vim as they would have under Bush; they downplayed the Obama administration's involvement in the botched "Fast and Furious" gun operation scandal; and members of the mainstream media openly mocked the right's anger over the administration's manipulation of the 2012

Benghazi terror attack. Obama had to be protected at all costs, including the cost of the media's credibility.

Meanwhile, the media savaged 2012 Republican presidential nominee Mitt Romney. They dug up a story from his high school days regarding him forcibly cutting a classmate's hair. They uncovered scandalous material about him strapping a dog to the roof of his car. They delved deep into his nefarious practice of investing in failing companies, and then cutting the dead weight to turn them around.

Then came Trump.

Trump didn't do anything aside from failing to comply with media's standards of behavior. He didn't pander to them or treat them with respect. And the media melted down. They treated Trump horribly, of course—but they'd already treated Bush and Romney just as badly. More importantly, the media lost their ability to pretend having standards of honesty and decency after selling their souls to the Obama White House. It was difficult to take their cries of incipient tyranny seriously after they bent over backward to flatter a White House that cracked down on reporters from Fox News and the Associated Press.

Why does any of this matter?

It matters because conservatives would be wise to understand that Trump didn't destroy the media; he inherited the shell of a media ready to crumble. He tapped the shell, and it fell apart. But that's not enough. Trump now has a golden opportunity to promulgate an alternative narrative in place of the one pushed by the discredited leftist media—if he can demonstrate credibility himself.

So far, he hasn't. And that means that his credibility will crumble at first contact from someone who hasn't already destroyed his or her credibility. Hence the media's renewed love for former FBI Director James Comey—they believe that they can restore their own credibility by watching him destroy Trump's.

Trump can do significant damage to the media, but only if he tells the truth. Now would be an excellent time to start.

What If There's No Trump-Putin Conspiracy?

July 12, 2017

This week, The New York Times dropped a potential bombshell: It alleged that Donald Trump Jr., then-Trump presidential campaign manager Paul Manafort and President Trump's son-in-law, Jared Kushner, met with a Russian government-linked lawyer in order to hear potential dirt about Hillary Clinton. The media immediately declared victory—this was obviously the first step toward establishing the Trump-Russia collusion about which they have crowed for nearly a year.

Meanwhile, Trump issued a series of tweets implying that he created a relationship of trust with Russian President Vladimir Putin, and that he might consider the foundation of a joint cybersecurity "unit" with the regime that allegedly attempted to influence the American election.

All of this looks rather suspicious, unless it turns out that pretty much every Trumpian scandal can be explained through a combination of Trump's ego and the incompetence of those around him.

Here's the truth: Even if every allegation surrounding Trump Jr., Manafort and Kushner regarding this meeting is true, that's *still* not evidence of any working relationship between the Trump campaign and the Russian government. At best, it's evidence that Trump Jr. and Co. weren't averse to attempts to feed them information. But as all accounts of the meeting state, no actual information was transferred, which means that there's *still* no Trump-Russia collusion.

What of Trump's bizarre behavior regarding Putin? The most obvious explanation isn't nefarious manipulation but pure, old-fashioned spite. Trump feels assaulted by the media who have been accusing him of being a Putin puppet since mid-2016. Rather than distancing himself from Putin, Trump's initial tendency is always to "punch back 10 times harder," as Melania Trump put it. That means embracing Putin, demonstrating a nonchalant apathy toward rumors and even treating Putin as a potential partner—after all, he has treated Trump more nicely than the media accusing him of corruption. From an egocentric perspective, Trump has more in common with Putin than he does with CNN.

That may be ugly, but it's also not collusion. It's not even in the same ballpark as then-President Obama promising "flexibility" to the Russians before the 2012 election.

This leaves the media short of the kill shot they've been implicitly promising for months. Ant that, in turn, makes the media desperate to prove that this hasn't all been a waste of time, a perverse attempt to find conspiracies in alphabet soup. And that means overplaying every single story into the Harbinger of Doom.

Here's the truth: Trump isn't a conspiratorial mastermind. He's a man irked by empty criticisms and dedicated to kicking his enemies in their most vulnerable areas. Sometimes that looks like he's reinforcing their theories. He isn't. So long as the media insist that Trump is someone he isn't, they'll keep finding conspiracies that don't fit the facts or the personality.

Democrats Know They Can Always Count on the Media

October 17, 2018

This week, Sen. Elizabeth Warren, D-Mass., in preparation for a 2020 presidential run, decided to fight back against President Trump's brutal nickname for her: Pocahontas. Trump, you'll recall, labeled her Pocahontas because for years, she has claimed Native American ancestry. Not only that, she claimed repeatedly that her mother's Native American ancestry drove her parents to elope after her father's family refused to welcome her mother with open arms thanks to their bigotry. As it turns out, Warren could never provide any evidence of Native American ancestry—even though she spent years labeling herself Native American while at the University of Pennsylvania Law School as well as Harvard Law School.

On Monday, Warren decided she'd had enough. She released a video of her family members discussing her claims of Native American background. "Native communities have faced discrimination, neglect and violence for generations," Warren intoned. "And Trump can say whatever he wants about me, but mocking Native Americans or any group in order to try to get at me? That's not what America stands for."

She accompanied that video with her supposed proof of Native American background: an analysis by professor Carlos Bustamante of Stanford University in which he explains that it is *possible* that Warren had a Native American ancestor anywhere from six to 10 generations ago. That would have made her anywhere from 1/64 to 1/1,024 Native American. The study was based not on Native American DNA but on Mexican, Peruvian and Colombian DNA.

In fact, not even Cherokees were happy with Warren. In a stunning rebuke, the Cherokee Nation released a statement saying, "Senator Warren is undermining tribal interests with her continued claims of tribal heritage," and that Warren's DNA test "makes a mockery out of DNA tests and its legitimate uses while also dishonoring legitimate tribal governments and their citizens, whose ancestors are well documented and whose heritage is proven."

All of this should have been foreseeable by anyone with half a brain. Falsely claiming you are Native American for years is bad enough. But releasing a study demonstrating that you are 99.9 percent white—and then claiming that such a study justifies your false claims? What made Warren, an intelligent human being, think such a thing?

Only one simple fact: Warren knows, as everyone in politics knows, that the media will cover for nearly any instance of leftist political manipulation. They'll cover for Warren fibbing about her ancestry. They'll cover for Texas Senate candidate Beto O'Rourke driving drunk, plowing into a truck and then attempting to flee the scene of the crime. They'll cover for Arizona Senate candidate Rep. Kyrsten Sinema saying that she didn't care if Americans joined the Taliban (CNN's headline: "Kyrsten Sinema's Anti-War Activist Past Under Scrutiny as She Runs for Senate"). Democrats have the enviable advantage of being able to trot out nearly any story and be given credibility by most of the mainstream media.

Non-Democrats, however, see this game. And every time the media simply parrot Democratic talking points on issues like Warren's ancestry, they undercut their credibility. Large media institutions have done more than anyone, including President Trump, to destroy their reputations with the American people. Their pathetic behavior over the past few weeks, in the approach to the 2018 elections, shows that they're doubling down on stupid.

The Scientific Experts Who Hate Science

January 9, 2019

This week, the American Psychological Association proved once again that it is a political body rather than a scientific one. This isn't the first time a major mental health organization has favored politics over science—in 2013, the American Psychiatric Association famously reclassified "gender identity disorder" in the Diagnostic and Statistical Manual of Mental Disorders, calling it "gender dysphoria" and then explaining that living with the delusion that you are a member of the opposite sex is not actually a mental disorder at all. That ruling was based on *zero* scientific evidence—much like the original DSM-5 classification of pedophilia as a "sexual orientation" before it was renamed "pedophilic disorder" under public pressure.

The latest example of the American Psychological Association's political hackery concerns the topic of "traditional masculinity." In the APA journal, it announced that it had released new guidelines to "help psychologists work with men and boys." Those guidelines suggest that "40 years of research" show that "traditional masculinity is psychologically harmful and that socializing boys to suppress their emotions causes damage that echoes both inwardly and outwardly." The APA explains that "traditional masculinity—marked by stoicism, competitiveness, dominance and aggression—is, on the whole, harmful. Men socialized in this way are less likely to engage in healthy behaviors."

Never mind that traditional masculinity—a masculinity geared toward channeling masculine instincts of building and protecting, rather than tearing down—built Western civilization and protected it from the brutalities of other civilizational forces. Never mind that traditional masculinity protected femininity and elevated women to equal status in public policy. Traditional masculinity is actually just men sitting around and eating burgers while grunting at one another about football, all the while crying on the inside because they have been prohibited by society from showing their feelings.

And it's worse than that. According to the APA, traditional masculinity bumps up "against issues of race, class and sexuality," maximizing both interior and exterior conflict. Dr. Ryon McDermott, a psychologist from the University of South Alabama who helped draft the new APA guidelines, suggested that gender is "no longer just this male-female binary." Rather, gender is a mere social construct that can be destroyed without consequence. Here's the APA making the extraordinarily dishonest statement that gender differences aren't biological *at all*, in contravention of all known social science research: "Indeed, when researchers strip away stereotypes and expectations, there isn't much difference in the basic behaviors of men and women."

Destroy masculinity in order to destroy discrimination and depression. Feminize men, and indoctrinate boys.

In order to reach this conclusion, the APA has to define traditional masculinity in the narrowest, most negative terms possible—and then other those who disagree as part of the patriarchy. But as a political body, the APA has little problem doing this.

All of this is not only nonsense; it's wildly counterproductive nonsense. Buried beneath the reams of nonsense in the APA report is this rather telling gem: "It's also important to encourage pro-social aspects of masculinity. ... In certain circumstances, traits like stoicism and self-sacrifice can be absolutely crucial." But we must never suggest that such traits ought to be included as part of a "traditional masculinity," because that would make some people feel excluded.

Here's the truth: Men are looking for meaning in a world that tells them they are perpetuators of discrimination and rape culture; that they are beneficiaries of an overarching, nasty patriarchy; that they are, at best, disposable partners to women, rather than protectors of them. Giving men purpose requires us to give them purpose *as men*, not merely as genderless beings. There's a lot to be said for the idea that our culture has ignored the necessity for men to become gentlemen. But that's a result of a left-wing culture that denigrates men, not a traditional masculinity built on the idea that men were born to defend, protect and build.

One thing is certainly true, though: The APA has destroyed itself on the shoals of politics. And there's no reason for honest-thinking people to take its anti-scientific pronouncements seriously simply because it masquerades as scientists while ignoring facts in favor of political correctness.

The Republican Pouncing Problem

February 13, 2019

In the past few weeks, prominent Democrats have endorsed infanticide; admitted to dressing in blackface; called for an end to fossil fuels, airplanes and farting cows; and trafficked in open anti-Semitism. None of this is a serious problem for many in the media. For members of the media, the *real* story is that Republicans keep pouncing.

Two weeks ago, Virginia Gov. Ralph Northam stated in an interview that he favors legislation that would allow a woman to abort a baby at the point of dilation and then added that in certain cases in which a baby would be born alive, the baby would be kept "comfortable" while parents and doctors decide what to do with it. This seems rather radical. Here was the Washington Post's take, as said in a headline: "Republicans seize on liberal positions to paint Democrats as radical." The positions, you see, are ackshually mainstream. It's just that Republicans *seized* on them and *painted* them as radical.

Last week, Rep. Alexandria Ocasio-Cortez, D-N.Y., released a Green New Deal backgrounder and FAQ on her website—and her staff sent the six-page document to a variety of media outlets. The document happens to be fully insane. It calls for America to be carbon emissions-free within 10 years without use of nuclear power. It suggests that every building in the country be either replaced or retrofitted. It calls for universal health care, free college education, replacement of airplanes with high-speed trains, replacement of "every combustion-engine vehicle," government-provided jobs, abolition of "farting cows" and, best of all, total "economic security" for anyone "unwilling to work." The proposal is so farcical that even Democrats ran from it screaming. AOC took down it down from her website and then deployed campaign aides to state that the document was "accidentally" released as an "early draft." Unsurprisingly, no revised draft has been posted.

Here is The New York Times' headline: "Ocasio-Cortez Team Flubs a Green New Deal Summary, and Republicans Pounce."

This week, Rep. Ilhan Omar, D-Minn., engaged in open anti-Semitism, suggesting that American support for Israel is "all about the Benjamins" and then doubling down on that comment by blaming the American Israel Public Affairs Committee for America's pro-Zionist attitude. This follows years of overtly anti-Semitic content from Omar, as well as from Rep. Rashida Tlaib, D-Mich., who suggested back in January that Americans who like Israel suffer from dual loyalty and "forgot which country they represent."

Politico tweeted: "The Republican Party has a new trio of Democratic villains: Rashida Tlaib, Ilhan Omar, and Alexandria Ocasio-Cortez."

Now, pouncing is never a story. Ever. It is a simple fact of politics that when people screw up, their political opponents react with alacrity. Highlighting that response rather than the underlying screw-up is the equivalent of a headline that reads "Sun Rises in Morning." Yet that's what the media do ... whenever Democrats screw up. Republican gaffes are a story in and of themselves. Democratic gaffes aren't a story; Republican nastiness is.

All of which demonstrates that a huge swath of the media is inseparable from the Democratic Party. If your first response to Democratic nut-jobbery is to get defensive about Republican blowback, you're no longer a journalist. You're merely a hack. You are, as President Trump would put it, "fake news"—an activist masquerading as a journalist.

I suppose this means I'm pouncing on the media, though.

Why We Don't Trust Our Institutions?

March 27, 2019

This week, special counsel Robert Mueller released his long-awaited report on alleged collusion between the Trump campaign and the Russian government to impact the 2016 election. His conclusion: no collusion. It's been apparent for quite some time that Mueller would end up here—every indictment has been based on an ancillary crime, not the chief question of election conspiracy. Nonetheless, the final result came as a bombshell.

That's because for two years, the mainstream media have treated Trump-Russian collusion as a reality. Facts would eventually arrive to fill in the gaps in the narrative. Surely, Trump's presidency would crumble when the deus ex machina, the Mueller report, arrived.

But that didn't happen. And so the media are left with unending egg on their faces, having suggested continuously for years that Trump was illegitimately elected, and that his campaign had engaged in treasonous activity to prevent the rightful president, Hillary Clinton, from assuming office.

That narrative found support in leaders from the Democratic intelligence community. Rep. Adam Schiff, D-Calif., of the House Intelligence Committee spent years camping outside CNN headquarters in a pup tent, ready at a moment's notice to suggest access to secret information that would certainly take down the president. Former CIA Director John Brennan accused Trump of treason, standing on his resume to do so. Former Director of National Intelligence James Clapper stated that Watergate "pales" beside allegations of coordination between the Trump campaign and Russia. Former acting FBI Director Andrew McCabe suggested that Trump could be a Russian cat's paw. Former FBI Director James Comey implied that Trump had fired him for nefarious reasons, not because Trump was angry with Comey for failing to announce that Trump wasn't under investigation.

Our intelligence leadership, in other words, humiliated themselves.

Meanwhile, in Chicago, Cook County prosecutors agreed to drop charges against alleged hate crime hoaxer Jussie Smollett, who alleged that he was beaten by two white men in the middle of the night on the streets of Chicago. Chicago Mayor Rahm Emanuel called the dropped charges a "whitewash." Chicago Police Superintendent Eddie Johnson bashed Smollett's defense team, explaining, "they chose to hide behind secrecy and broker a deal to circumvent the judicial system."

Why have key institutions betrayed their initial mission? Mission creep. The job of the media is to objectively cover stories, not to drive narratives. The job of the intelligence community is to diligently follow evidence, not to follow its cognitive bias. The job of the state's attorney is to prosecute crime, not to play politics.

Without defined roles, our institutions crumble. Treating institutions as mere tools to be wielded in pursuit of some higher goal leads to the destruction of those institutions; they become little more than weapons, aimed by those in power. That's dangerous stuff. We should be able to trust our press. If we can't, then we can no longer base our republican decision-making on a common set of facts. We should be able to trust our intelligence community and our prosecutors. If we can't, then we can't support granting them the power they require to protect us.

But protecting institutions has taken a back seat to do-goodism. "Objective" journalists see themselves as crusaders; political members of the intelligence community see themselves as protectors; prosecutors see themselves as emissaries of social justice rather than as part of a broader, more objective system of determining guilt and innocence. Institutions only mean more than the people who comprise them when the people who comprise them value the institutions more than their own politics. That's being lost. The result is the continued atomization of our society.

The Media/Democrat Complex Strikes Big Tech

June 12, 2019

This week, The New York Times ran a massive piece detailing the supposed radicalization of one Caleb Cain. Cain moved from political liberalism toward self-ascribed "tradcon" status from watching YouTube videos. The New York Times charted this nefarious move by following those videos. The suggestion by The Times was simple: If you watch typical conservative content hosted by people like me, you will eventually end up watching material hosted by alt-right figures. The only solution, presumably, would be for YouTube to downgrade material The Times dislikes.

This attitude isn't only springing from The Times. Axios chief technology correspondent Ina Fried grilled Google CEO Sundar Pichai over the weekend, essentially demanding that YouTube do something to marginalize videos Fried dislikes. Vox ran a full-scale propaganda campaign last week to get conservative comedian Steven Crowder kicked off YouTube for the great sin of making offensive jokes about one of Vox's columnists. Taking their cues from Democratic leaders like House Speaker Nancy Pelosi, various media outlets have spent years suggesting that Facebook's unwillingness to censor political materials led to Hillary Clinton's unjustifiable 2016 presidential defeat.

And it's not just targeting big tech companies. The far-left organization Media Matters for America routinely leads boycott attempts against advertisers who deign to sponsor conservative programs—even if those advertisers sponsor a wide variety of political programming. Pseudojournalists from organizations like Vox and Huffington Post spend their days calling advertisers for comment on various controversial statements by right-wing hosts from Tucker Carlson to Laura Ingraham to Sean Hannity. Their goal isn't to follow the news but to generate a wave of advertiser-pullout announcements likely to do damage to those conservative hosts.

Such censoriousness is rarely, if ever, practiced on the political right. YouTube and Facebook and Twitter are never targeted by conservatives over their unwillingness to shut down opposing points of view; they're criticized for their willingness to kowtow to the political left and its demands for speech suppression. Advertisers on left-wing programming can speak freely, secure in the knowledge that conservatives won't be calling them up to rip them for sponsoring shows like Rachel Maddow's.

That's good. That's how it should be. But for members of the political left, it isn't.

There are two reasons for that. The first is obvious: Those on the political left long ago abandoned the traditional liberal notion that those who disagree have a right to speak. Instead, they must be deplatformed and their advertisers punished, lest their nefarious ideas spread and metastasize. "Repressive tolerance," in the parlance of Herbert Marcuse, has become a mainstay of left-wing thinking.

The other reason is far more cynical: Many in the media want a regeneration of the monopolistic media control of the past. They long for the days when everyone consumed mainstream product to the exclusion of alternative sources. It's no coincidence that YouTube and Facebook have been touting their elevation of "authoritative" news in recent years—they're looking to appease a ravenous media eager to tear them down.

The media and Democrats have picked the right target: The lords of Big Tech are eager to please and frightened of blowback. They're political liberals who can be intimidated into censorship while being simultaneously assured that they're making the world a better place.

They aren't. All it would take for this censorious moment to end would be a little backbone: Facebook, YouTube and Twitter announcing that they won't censor people unless those people violate actual First Amendment principles like incitement and libel; advertisers announcing that they won't pull their dollars based on astroturfed pressure tactics. But backbone is in short supply. And the glut of intimidation won't relax anytime soon.

New Wave of Feminism

Feminism is the ability to choose what you want to do.
—Nancy Reagan

The Left's Vagina-Based Politics Demeans Women

January 15, 2017

Last Saturday, in an attempt to demonstrate outrage at ... at ... well, at *something*, some three million people across the country, mostly women, participated in women's marches. The scattershot platform for the march included public funding for contraception and abortion, equal pay, protections for illegal immigrants, anti-Israel activism and taxpayer-subsidized tampons, among other disparate causes. What united them? Hatred for the reality that Donald Trump was sworn in as president of the United States on Friday.

Two contrasting images emerged from the march itself: first, people filling the streets out of pure, unadulterated but vaguely motivated frustration; second, some of the most egregiously perverse speeches and signage in modern political history. While the left celebrated the first image—isn't this a sign of a political uprising in the making?—it ignored the second image, which is far more likely to backfire than to generate enthusiasm.

That second image was promulgated by celebrities like Ashley Judd, who was once considered a frontrunner for the Democratic nomination for the Senate in Kentucky. The has-been actress raged: "I am a nasty woman. ... I didn't know devils could be resurrected, but I feel Hitler in these streets. A mustache traded for a toupee. ... I am nasty like the bloodstains on my bed sheets. We don't actually choose if and when to have our periods. Believe me, if we could, some of us would. We do not like throwing away our favorite pairs of underpants. Tell me, why are pads and tampons still taxed when Viagra and Rogaine are not?"

Meanwhile, thousands of women donned "p----hats," or pink knit caps with cat ears, designed to rebuke Trump for the "Access Hollywood" tape in which he said he could grab women "by the p----" and get away with it. They marched with signs reading, "Leave

My P---- Alone" and "If abortion is murder then b---jobs are cannibalism" and "This P---- Bites And She Slays." NARAL Pro-Choice America handed out signs with similar messages.

This reduction of women to their constituent body parts is particularly ironic coming from the same side of the political aisle that declares that men sometimes have vaginas and that some women have penises. But more importantly, reducing female priorities to killing babies and increased funding for maxi pads merely objectifies women. Instead of recognizing that women have all sorts of political views, instead of recognizing that many women believe that they ought to be left alone by government in order to pursue their dreams, the women's marches declared that government has to treat vaginal possession with a sort of victim status, deserving of special protection.

The suggestion that the government must guarantee special privileges for women because their biology makes them somehow lesser, or that abortion rights are necessary to achieve equality, reduces the fight for female equality to the fight for female *sameness*. That's insulting to women.

And it's off-putting to voters. If these women are so concerned about vulgarity, why do they embrace it? If they're so upset that Trump supposedly reduces women to body parts, why promote that same silly thinking?

The left tried to run on the War on Women in 2016 and lost. Now they're doubling down. But apparently, so long as they can pat themselves on the back for their unearned moral superiority, they'll be happy.

The Insanity of the Left's Child Gender-Confusion Agenda

April 12, 2017

On Sunday, The New York Times ran a piece by Jack Turban, a research fellow at the Yale School of Medicine. Turban says that doctors should begin applying puberty blockers to children who identify as transgender as early as possible. That's because, according to him, "it has become clear that if we support these children in their transgender identities instead of trying to change them, they thrive instead of struggling with anxiety and depression."

Turban uses as his example one 14-year-old girl named Hannah who was born a boy named Jonah. Turban glows: "Hannah is using a puberty-blocking implant and getting ready to embark on the path of developing a female body by starting estrogen. Ten years ago most doctors would have called this malpractice. New data has now made it the protocol for thousands of American children."

Ten years ago, doctors weren't embracing politically correct insanity as medicine.

Turban, you see, claims that by transforming children's bodies younger, we will help them avoid societal stigma, and that it's that stigma that's responsible for the shockingly high rates of suicide and depression associated with gender dysphoria. But there's no hard data to support that notion. A study from professors at the American Foundation for Suicide Prevention and the Williams Institute at the UCLA School of Law, for example, found that 46 percent of transgender men and 42 percent of transgender women in the study had attempted suicide.

Is this due to discrimination? The study does show high levels of discrimination against transgender people. But it *also* shows that the suicide rate among transgender women who say people identify them as transgender regularly is 45 percent. How about those who are able to pass for the gender to which they claim membership? Their suicide rate is *still 40 percent*. How about the suicide rate among those transgender individuals who have had hormone treatment? It's 45 percent. Surgery doesn't militate against suicide either.

But Turban has an agenda. And so, he cites one study of 63 transgender children, which found that if they were allowed to "socially transition"—if people treated them as their preferred sex—then they had indistinguishable levels of anxiety and depression from that of their peers. But this study concerns children, who have not yet experienced the rigors of sex drive and sexual dynamics; it also ignores the small sample size and the fact that a reported 8 in 10 children who experience gender confusion grow out of it. But Turban's fine with maintaining gender confusion for those 8 children out of 10 in order to preserve Hannah's peace of mind—even if Hannah might have grown out of her symptoms herself, thereby lowering risk of suicide over time.

This is science with an agenda.

Adults should be free to make decisions about their sexuality and their bodies. But children should not be subjected to the whims of politically driven adults when it comes to massive bodily mutilation that impairs function for a lifetime—all before the child has experienced puberty. And society should not be obligated to obey the gender theory nonsense of the radical left, which seeks to confuse as many children as possible in the name of an anti-biological program in service to a political agenda.

No, You're Not a Bigot If You Only Want to Have Sex With People to Which You Are Attracted

May 24, 2017

You. Yes, you. You're a bigot.

Are you a straight man who only wants to have sex with women? Are you a gay man who only wants to have sex with men? Are you a bisexual man who wants to have sex with people of both sexes but only if they are good-looking? Are you asexual?

You're a bigot.

According to Samantha Allen of The Daily Beast, it is deeply "disappointing but unsurprising" that under 20 percent of Americans in a recent survey said they would be open to having sex with a transgender person. That's because, she says, "Cultural acceptance has tended to lag behind formal recognition."

It turns out that according to the left, all sexual behavior is malleable and based largely on social structures that have been implemented by the patriarchy. Men and women don't exist but for their self-perception—we know that a man can be a woman and a woman can be a man, regardless of biology. That's why Caitlyn Jenner isn't just a man with a mental disorder and some plastic surgery and hormone injections; Caitlyn Jenner is as much of a woman as Michelle Obama. The left reasons that if a man can be a woman, then a man who only wants to have sex with biological women must be a bigot—his desires have been wrongly defined by a society that restricted the definition of womanhood to, you know, women. If only men had been exposed to the deeper truth of gender earlier. If only they'd known that some women have male genitalia. Then, perhaps they'd be willing to have sex with biological men who are actually women.

The same holds true with regard to homosexuals, of course. If a woman is a lesbian, it's discriminatory of her to not want to have sex with a man who identifies as a woman. Her desires have also been shaped by her environment. And her environment has drawn a stark but wrong—oh, ever so wrong!—line between biological men and biological women.

If all of this sounds insane, that's because it is. Straight men are attracted to women, not men who identify as women. Straight women are attracted to biological men. As a general rule, homosexuals are attracted to members of the same biological sex. Attempting to pretend away reality doesn't change that reality.

But the left is plagued by two myths that lie in direct opposition to one another. The first: All human behavior can be changed by changing society at large. The second: All human sexual behavior is innate and unchanging. Under the first myth, if we just train people that men and women are the same and that even their genitals don't provide a meaningful difference, men will begin having sex with transgender women, and women will begin having sex with transgender men. Under the second myth, however, transgender identity itself is immutable and unchanging, as is homosexuality and heterosexuality. This provides an unanswerable conundrum for transgender advocates: How can they get people to accept transgender people sexually when people's sexuality is supposedly unchanging?

So the left merely ignores the problem and papers it over with the word "bigot."

Reality isn't bigotry. People are attracted to those they are attracted to. There is a biological component to that as well as a cultural component. But ignoring biology in favor of culture is idiotic, and ignoring culture in favor of biology is ignorant. They both play a part. The suggestion that discriminatory nastiness is at the root of the perfectly logical biological desire for people to have sex with members of the opposite biological sex is merely a slur, a crutch to cover up the illogic of the far left when it comes to gender and sex.

The Sultans of America and Their Harems

November 22, 2017

Americans have been buried in the last six weeks by a blizzard of reports of sexual harassment, assault, misconduct and malfeasance from our politicians, journalists and Hollywood glitterati. In the last week alone, we've seen a picture of Sen. Al Franken, D-Minn., during his pre-senatorial days placing his hands over a sleeping woman's breasts; the suspension of New York Times journalist Glenn Thrush for allegedly harassing young female journalists; and eight women telling the Washington Post that fabled television host Charlie Rose had made unwanted sexual advances ranging from groping to lewd phone calls. That follows on the heels of allegations of child molestation against Alabama Senate Republican nominee Roy Moore, confirmed accusations of unwanted exposure from comedian Louis C.K. and allegations of sexual assault against Russell Simmons. Every day, it seems, a new member of the cultural aristocracy comes tumbling down.

What's behind all of it? Why did it take so long for this avalanche to start? And what does it tell us about the culture we've built?

Misconduct thrives when accountability fades. Historically speaking, we have always had elite classes of people who engaged in sexually atrocious behavior, and that class was largely confined to those with power and their hangers-on. Kings and potentates could revel in their harems—they could seize and rape concubines—and those upon whom they bestowed favor could expect to enjoy like treatment. But in an egalitarian, free society, a society without hereditary aristocracy, we pride ourselves on having a common standard of behavior for everyone.

That's simply not true. When it comes to sexual exploitation of women in particular, we treat our new aristocracy in the same way peasants treated the old aristocracy: with deference. In America, three things confer aristocratic status: fame, money and power. Hollywood, politics and journalism are built on all three. And elite status in each of those industries bought not just a bevy of opportunities for brutality but also a silent knowledge that the consequences would be slight for engaging in that brutality.

First, the opportunities. Just as certain peasants of old sought to curry favor with lords, too many Americans seek to curry favor with the powerful. That's the story of the Hollywood casting couch. It's the story of the famed journalist and his nighttime corner booth at the local pub. It's the story of the politician and his late-night office meetings. Does anyone think women were dying to meet Harvey Weinstein or Charlie Rose or Glenn Thrush? Each story we hear tells the same tale: Women thought the only way they could get ahead was to treat these men with complaisance. They thought that they couldn't turn down dinner invites. And if they were abused, they thought they had to keep their mouths shut.

In many cases, they did. That's because the public offered no consequences to the elite. Perhaps we blamed the victims and were unwilling to blame the accusers. Perhaps the darkest side of humanity revels in the pain inflicted by others. Whatever the case, the aristocrats knew, and they acted accordingly.

So, what's changed now? It's tempting to say that we've woken up—that we're unwilling to allow fame and money and power to excuse abuse, and we're not going to go back to the old way anymore. But that would be too sanguine. So long as fame and money and power exist, there will be those who seek to exploit them and those who look the other way. False idols always have their adherents.

It's our job to ensure that the idols remain smashed. And that means recanting our own idolatry for a cultural sultanate that deserves to be torn down.

Does Yes Ever Mean Yes?

December 20, 2017

Over the weekend, Jessica Bennett, gender editor of The New York Times—yes, that's a real title—wrote a piece titled "When Saying 'Yes' Is Easier Than Saying 'No'." She argued that in many cases, women say yes to sex but actually don't want to do so: "Sometimes 'yes' means 'no,' simply because it is easier to go through with it than explain our way out of the situation. Sometimes 'no' means 'yes,' because you actually *do* want to do it, but you know you're not *supposed to* lest you be labeled a slut. And if you're a man, that 'no' often means 'just try harder'—because, you know, persuasion is part of the game." Bennett continues by arguing that consent is actually societally defined, that "our idea of what we want—of our own desire—is linked to what we think we're *supposed* to want."

But Bennett offers no clear solutions to this issue. If it's true that women say yes but mean no, are men supposed to read minds? If a woman says no but a man seduces her until she says yes, is the initial no supposed to take precedence over the final yes?

Unfortunately, Bennett offers no guidance. Neither does Rebecca Reid, who wrote in Metro UK that she once participated in a threesome because she "didn't want to be rude." And Reid says that such experiences aren't uncommon: "There are hundreds of reasons why, but they all boil down to the same thing. We're nice girls. We've been raised to be nice." She adds: "sometimes being careful means having sex that you don't want, that leaves you feeling dirty and sad and a bit icky. It's not rape. It's not abuse. But it's not nice, either."

In the pages of The New Yorker, a similarly vague story went viral. Titled "Cat Person," it describes a woman named Margot who seduces a man and sends him all the signals that she wants to have sex with him but is internally divided over whether to go through with it: "she knew that her last chance of enjoying this encounter had disappeared, but that she would carry through with it until it was over." In the end, she cuts short their relationship, and he texts that she is a "Whore."

It's a painful story, to be sure. But it also raises a serious question: What exactly are men supposed to do in such scenarios? Because as a society, we're beyond suggesting that women are doing anything wrong in consenting to nonmarital sex; women are free to do what they want. But we *are* in the midst of a push to punish male aggressors. And if we water down consent to nothingness, how can we ever expect men to feel safe in the knowledge that a sexual encounter won't come with life-altering implications?

Perhaps the problem is expectations. All three articles articulate the complaint that women want to fulfill men's expectations. But none of them admit to another expectation, one created by the feminist movement: the expectation that women themselves must treat sex casually or fall prey to reinforcing the patriarchy. Ask a person of traditional moral standards whether the woman should have said no in all of these stories. The answer will be yes. But then that person will be regarded as a prude.

There are costs to societal expectations. Traditional mores ruled out the male expectation of sex in non-commitment scenarios. Yes, men had hopes of sex—all men do, virtually all of the time. But men had no expectation that such hopes would be achieved absent serious commitment. Thanks to our consent-only society, however, in which sexual activity is a throwaway and any notion of cherishing it is scoffed at as patriarchal, men have developed expectations that too many women feel they must meet—and men have taken up the feminist standard that consent is a goal to be achieved. The cost to such a system is borne almost entirely by women.

The healthiest system of sexual interaction is a system in which most women can be sure enough of themselves most of the time to feel decent after saying yes. That system no longer exists, thanks to the disconnect between commitment and sex. And the continuing disconnect between consent and expectation will continue to burden women in heavier and heavier ways.

The Virtue-Signaling Anti-Virtue Crowd

January 10, 2018

Imagine it's late 2011. The world just found out about Jerry Sandusky, former assistant Penn State football coach who would be convicted of repeatedly raping children in 2012. Penn State higher-ups, in an attempt to turn the focus of the scandal away from the school, decide to turn an annual banquet into a celebration of those fighting child rape. They call up head coach Joe Paterno. They call up President Graham Spanier. They call up athletic director Tim Curley. All of them give long, brave speeches about the evils of sexual exploitation of children resulting in rousing applause from all the Penn State boosters. All the attendees wear pins showing their solidarity with molestation victims. The event is nationally televised.

You'd be disgusted, wouldn't you? You'd think to yourself, "Perhaps it isn't a good idea for a school that just became nationally renowned for one of the worst sex scandals in modern American history to preach about its commitment to the kiddies."

Now fast-forward to 2018. It's been only a few months since we found out that Hollywood megaproducer Harvey Weinstein allegedly raped multiple women, sexually abused other women and sexually harassed still more women. Each day, more and more prominent men are caught up in the net of #MeToo, the national movement to listen to the stories of abused women: Matt Lauer, Kevin Spacey, Charlie Rose, Russell Simmons, Jeffrey Tambor, Andrew Kreisberg, Louis C.K., Ed Westwick, Brett Ratner, Dustin Hoffman, Jeremy Piven, Danny Masterson and James Toback.

Yet on Sunday, Hollywood held itself a festival of virtue-signaling at the Golden Globes. All the women dressed in black in homage to the victims of a sexual harassment epidemic that has plagued Hollywood since the inception of the casting couch. The men wore "Time's Up" buttons to show solidarity. Oprah Winfrey, who was once quite close with Weinstein, gave an emotional speech in which she likened modern-day victims of sexual abuse to a black woman raped by six white men in 1944 Alabama. The cameras cut away to Meryl Streep, who once praised Weinstein as a "god" and gave a standing ovation to accused child rapist Roman Polanski. The entire crowd cheered its goodwill approximately six years after the Hollywood Foreign Press Association gave a lifetime achievement award to Woody Allen, who was credibly accused of molesting his own stepdaughter when she was 7 years old.

All of this was supposed to make us feel that Hollywood is somehow leading the charge against sexual aggression. But that's simply not true. Hollywood isn't doing anything to materially change its culture; it's simply operating out of fear of public scrutiny. When the spotlight moves on, people in Hollywood will go right back to doing what they've been doing for years: exploiting people less powerful than them. Winfrey had nothing to say about sexual misconduct in Hollywood for 30 years, even though she was the Queen of All Media; treating her as some sort of beacon of light now is simply ridiculous.

America knows posturing when it sees it. And what we're seeing now isn't bravery.

Stop Feministsplaining Sex to Men

January 17, 2018

There's a word that has become popular in feminist circles these days: "mansplaining." The word is a mashup of "man" and "explaining" and refers to men who condescendingly explain the facts of life to women. So, for example, if a man believes a woman doesn't understand directions and slowly repeats those directions to a woman, he's mansplaining and, therefore, guilty of cruelty and stupidity.

Well, feminists, it's time to stop "feministsplaining" sex to men.

The #MeToo movement has been good for America. It's good that women who have been sexually assaulted and abused are coming forward; it's good that we're finally having conversations about the nature of consent and the problems with a casual hookup culture that obfuscates sexual responsibility. But the #MeToo movement hasn't stopped there. Men are now being pilloried for the sin of taking women too literally—of not reading women's minds.

Take, for example, "Grace," an anonymous woman who went on a rotten date with comedian Aziz Ansari. According to Grace, Ansari treated her abominably: He took her to dinner, gave her white wine instead of red, pushed her to come to his apartment and then engaged in a vigorous round of sexual activities to which she apparently consented. She eventually said no—and when she did, he stopped. Later, she suggested that Ansari hadn't obeyed her "non-verbal cues"—nonverbal cues that reportedly included undressing and then voluntarily servicing Ansari.

In the aftermath, Grace felt used. So she texted Ansari, explaining to him that she felt terrible about the date. "I want to make sure you're aware so maybe the next girl doesn't have to cry on the ride home," she said.

This is feministsplaining sex. Here's the problem: The condescension isn't earned. From Grace's story, it seems she was less than clear in her nonverbal communications but she wanted Ansari to read her mind—and that when he didn't, she therefore had leeway to lecture him about his sins and, more broadly, those of all men.

It's not just Grace. Rachel Thompson of Mashable explained: "The responses to the woman's story are peppered with the word 'should.' She *should* have said no ... For many women, uttering an explicit 'no' is not as easy or straightforward as you might think." Well, as it turns out, reading minds is not quite as easy or straightforward as feminists might think. It was feminists who boiled down sexual relations to the issue of consent. Traditionalists always argued that physical intimacy and emotional intimacy ought to be linked. But they were accused of removing female agency with such linkage and condemned for "mansplaining."

How about this: no feministsplaining and no mansplaining when it comes to sex? How about we instead focus on communication between men and women? How about sexual partners demand more from one another than physical release so they aren't disappointed that they're being treated as sex objects? A system prizing love and commitment doesn't require nearly the amount of explanation as a system that dispenses with both.

When Abortion Becomes a Sacrament

July 11, 2018

This week, amid widespread Democratic tumult regarding the selection of a replacement for Supreme Court Justice Anthony Kennedy, alleged comedian Michelle Wolf paid tribute to the most important facet of American life: abortion. On her Netflix show on Sunday, Wolf dressed up in red, white and blue, and shrieked into the camera, "God bless abortions, and God bless America!" She explained: "Women, if you need an abortion, get one! If you want an abortion, get one! ... And women, don't forget: You have the power to give life and men will try to control that. Don't let them!"

Along with that inane outburst, she justified abortion itself. "Look," she stated, "access to abortion is good and important. Some people say abortion is killing a baby. It's not. It's stopping a baby from happening."

Well, some people say Michelle Wolf is killing comedy. She's not. She's stopping comedy from happening.

But more importantly, a ground shift has taken place in how Democrats think about abortion. Back in 2005, I wrote that the Democratic "safe, legal and rare" formulation regarding abortion was logically and morally untenable: If Democrats wanted abortion to be rare thanks to its inherent immorality, there was no reason for it to be legal. Democrats have finally come around: They're now "shouting" their abortions, proclaiming them from the rooftops, suggesting that there is a moral *good* achieved by abortion.

Thus, Lena Dunham said just two years ago, "I still haven't had an abortion, but I wish I had." Thus, Chelsea Handler, who has had two abortions, explained in the pages of Playboy, "I don't ever look back and think, 'God, I wish I'd had that baby.'" Her article was accompanied by a picture of a woman's hand with a raised middle finger with a pink bow around it; attached to the bow is a small card that reads, "It's an abortion!"

Yes, abortion is now a signifier that you refuse to be ruled by the patriarchy. Avoidance of pregnancy may be a wise life choice, according to third-wave feminists, preventing women from being sucked into the grinding maw of maternal life. But abortion is something even better: a signal that you just don't care about the system. The system demands that if you're pregnant with a child, you make your own concerns secondary; the system must be fought.

Gloria Steinem once remarked, "If men could get pregnant, abortion would be a sacrament." But modern-day feminists have determined that abortion *is* a sacrament specifically *because* women can get pregnant: Showing that control over your body even extends to the killing of your unborn child is a way of standing up against patriarchal concerns with women as the source of future generations.

For Michelle Wolf, abortion isn't just another decision. It's a giant middle finger to the moral establishment. And those who would fight abortion are desacralizing the mysterious holiness of a ritual that reinforces women's control. No wonder Wolf thinks God blesses abortion; abortion is her god.

The Politicization of the Kavanaugh Sexual Abuse Allegations Damages #MeToo

September 19, 2018

This week, Judge Brett Kavanaugh was hit with accusations of sexual abuse from Christine Blasey Ford, a professor at Palo Alto University. According to Ford, some 36 years ago, when Kavanaugh was 17 and she was 15, Kavanaugh took her into a room at a pool party—along with another high school classmate, Mark Judge—and then proceeded to lie on top of her and try to disrobe her, even putting his hand over her mouth to prevent her from screaming.

These are serious allegations. Kavanaugh has denied them completely. He denies he was at such a pool party; he denies he has ever engaged in such behavior. Ford, for her part, only came forward months after sending letters to Sen. Dianne Feinstein, D-Calif., and Rep. Anna Eshoo, D-Calif., and contacting the Washington Post. She originally didn't want to reveal her name or her story. Feinstein didn't ask Kavanaugh about it in writing, or in closed or open hearings; she didn't inform her fellow Democratic senators about the allegations; now she's reportedly attempting to prevent Republican senators from asking questions of Ford.

So, how in the hell is Kavanaugh supposed to defend himself?

This has always been the key question the #MeToo movement has adamantly refused to answer: What should the standard of proof, or even the standard of believability, be? Should the standard be criminal liability? Presumably not, since most accusers are emerging to speak long after alleged incidents. Should the standard be credibility of the individual telling the story combined with supporting details that lend additional credibility? Perhaps, but that apparently isn't enough for some. The standard promoted by many in the #MeToo movement is the far-too-simplistic and outright dangerous "believe all women" standard. By that standard, former

President Bill Clinton is a rapist. So are the Duke lacrosse players, the members of a University of Virginia frat house and a foreign exchange Columbia University student—all of whom were exonerated.

Kavanaugh's accuser didn't tell anyone about the incident at the time; she didn't go to the police. Her first retelling of the story came in 2012, three decades after the alleged incident, in a spousal counseling session with a therapist. She told the Washington Post that she doesn't remember key details of the night in question. She doesn't remember the location or how she got there or the date. The notes of her therapist conflict with her statements about the evening.

There are real questions to be asked about her account—and about Feinstein's political maneuvering. But instead, many on the left insist that the "believe all women" standard be applied to accusers against those on the right but that the general credibility standard should be applied to their own favorites. That's nonsensical, and insulting. What's more, it deliberately undermines the bulwark of universal approval with which #MeToo should be met. We should all be able to agree that some standard beyond mere belief is required here—and we should all be willing to hear evidence that implicates our favorite political figures. But if we insist on applying a politically motivated double standard in the name of #MeToo, the support for #MeToo will crumble.

That would be a tragedy, but it would also be a familiar tragedy. All too often, movements that should draw broad public support are undermined by fringe cases used as clubs by members of politically driven groups. We should all agree that any racist police shootings must be stopped—but such agreement falls apart when some insist that questionable shootings be treated as racist shootings. We should all agree that sexual abuse must be stopped—but such agreement disintegrates when some insist that unsubstantiated sexual abuse allegations be treated just like substantiated allegations.

Politics should not be allowed to override basic human decency. Yet again, that's what's happening.

No, Abortion Isn't a Constitutional Right

May 22, 2019

In the past several weeks, a bevy of states have passed extensive new restrictions on abortion. Alabama has effectively banned abortion from point of conception. Georgia has banned abortion from the time a heartbeat is detected, as have Ohio, Kentucky and Mississippi. Missouri has banned abortion after eight weeks. Other states are on the move as well.

This has prompted paroxysms of rage from the media and the political left—the same folks who celebrated when New York passed a law effectively allowing abortion up until point of birth and who defended Virginia Gov. Ralph Northam's perverse statements about late-term abortion. According to these thinkers, conservatives have encroached on a supposed "right to abortion" inherent in the Constitution.

This, of course, is a lie. There is no "right to abortion" in the Constitution. The founders would have been appalled by such a statement. The Supreme Court's decision in Roe v. Wade (1973) is a legal monstrosity by every available metric: As legal scholar John Hart Ely wrote, Roe "is not constitutional law and gives almost no sense of an obligation to try to be." The court's rationale is specious; the court relied on the ridiculous precedent in Griswold v. Connecticut (1965) that a broad "right to privacy" can be crafted from "penumbras, formed by emanations." Then the court extended that right to privacy to include the killing of a third party, an unborn human life—and overrode state definitions of human life in the process.

How? The court relied on the self-contradictory notion of "substantive due process"—the belief that a law can be ruled unconstitutional under the Fifth and 14th amendments so long as the court doesn't like the substance of the law. That's asinine, obviously.

The due process provision of both amendments was designed to ensure that state and federal government could not remove life, liberty or property without a sufficient legal process, *not* to broadly allow courts to strike down state definitions of conduct that justify removal of life, liberty and property. As Justice Clarence Thomas has written, "The Fourteenth Amendment's Due Process Clause is not a 'secret repository of substantive guarantees against "unfairness."'"

Nonetheless, the notion that such a right to abortion is enshrined in America's moral fabric has taken hold among the intelligentsia. Thus, we now experience the odd spectacle of those on the political left declaring that the Constitution enshrines a right to abortion—yet does not include a right to bear arms, a right to freedom of political speech, a right to retain property free of government seizure or a right to practice religion.

For much of the left, then, the term "constitutional right" has simply come to mean "thing I want." And that is incredibly dangerous, given that the power of the judiciary springs not from legislative capacity but from supposed interpretive power. Judges are not supposed to read things into the Constitution but to properly read the Constitution itself. The use of the judiciary as a club has led to a feeling of radical frustration among Americans; it has radically exacerbated our culture gap.

The legislative moves in Alabama and other states will open a much-needed debate about the role of the states, the role of legislatures and the role of government. All of that is good for the country. Those who insist, however, that the Supreme Court act as a mechanism for their political priorities are of far more danger to the country than that debate.

Beyond Borders

"The world must learn to work together, or finally it will not work at all."
— Dwight Eisenhower

Time to Defund the United Nations

December 27, 2017

Last week, Democrats and many in the mainstream media became highly perturbed by the Trump administration's suggestion that the United States might tie continued foreign aid to support for its agenda abroad. Foreign dictators agreed. Turkish President Recep Tayyip Erdogan, who spent the last year arresting dissidents, announced, "Mr. Trump, you cannot buy Turkey's democratic free will with your dollars, our decision is clear."

Herein lies the great irony of the United Nations: While it's the Mos Eisley of international politics—a hive of scum and villainy—and it votes repeatedly to condemn the United States and Israel, the tyrannies that constitute the body continue to oppress their own peoples. Among those who voted last week to condemn the U.S. for recognizing Jerusalem as Israel's capital and moving its embassy to Jerusalem were North Korea, Iran, Yemen and Venezuela. Why exactly should the United States *ever* take advice from those nations seriously?

We shouldn't. And we should stop sending cash to an organization that operates as a front for immoral agenda items.

The United Nations spends the vast majority of its time condemning Israel: According to UN Watch, the U.N. Human Rights Council issued 135 resolutions from June 2006 to June 2016, 68 of which were against Israel; the U.N. Educational, Scientific and Cultural Organization *only* passes resolutions against Israel; and the U.N. General Assembly issued 97 resolutions from 2012 through 2015, 83 of which targeted Israel.

Meanwhile, the U.N. has done nearly nothing with regard to Syria. It has instead suggested that Israel turn over the Golan Heights to the Syrian regime. The U.N. can't even successfully prevent the slaughter of the Rohingya in Myanmar. But they certainly have something say about whether the United States ought to recognize Jerusalem as Israel's capital.

One of the great lies of the Obama administration was that diplomacy is a foreign policy. We often heard from it that the only two alternatives were diplomacy and war. That was the stated reason for pursuing a one-sided nuclear deal with Iran that left Iran with burgeoning regional power and legitimacy. "What? Do you want a war or something?" it asked.

But the moment that the Trump administration uses tools of diplomacy, including financial pressure, to achieve American ends, the left complains. Would it prefer war? Diplomacy is a tool, not a foreign policy, and the use of diplomacy to pressure other nations to follow our lead is not only smart but also necessary. That is why the Trump administration was exactly right to negotiate a $285 million cut to the U.N.'s budget. Now we ought to slash our contributions to the counterproductive organization, since we pay one-fifth of the total bill.

The U.N. has always been a foolish fantasy, a League of Nations knockoff that's been about as productive and twice as irritating. It's an outmoded organization that's outlived whatever small usefulness it once had. There's no reason for us to continue cutting checks to prop up regimes that condemn us publicly for exercising the most basic standards of morality.

Who Controls Your Kids' Lives?

April 25, 2018

Former Republican Sen. Phil Gramm of Texas was fond of telling a story about his time stumping for educational change. "My educational policies are based on the fact that I care more about my children than you do," Gramm once said to a woman. "No, you don't," she replied. "OK," said Gramm. "What are their names?"

Gramm's fundamental premise is inalterably correct: Parents care more about their children than do the members of the bureaucracy. But parents are being gradually curbed in their authority by precisely those bureaucrats across the West.

On Tuesday, a British court condemned a not-yet-2-year-old child to die. Now, make no mistake: The child, Alfie Evans, is expected to die in the near future anyway; he suffers from an undiagnosed brain condition that has robbed him of much of his function. But his parents simply wanted to be able to transfer him from a British hospital to an Italian hospital to seek experimental care.

And the British court system refused.

Citing the expertise of Evans' doctors, the courts declared that Evans' best interests are not served by his parents' attempts to save his life. Instead, the little boy would be deprived of life support, left to die without oxygen or water. The ruling, the judge said, "represents the final chapter in the life of this extraordinary little boy." But that chapter was written by the British bureaucracy, not by his parents—the ones who will have to engrave his epitaph and visit his grave.

This appalling result isn't the first of its kind; just last year, a little boy named Charlie Gard was taken off life support thanks to the British court system, which presented his parents from sending him to the United States for further treatment. Again, the courts made the argument that the best interest of the child lay in his death.

All of this is the final result of a system of thought that places parental control of children below the expertise of bureaucrats on the scale of priorities. It's one thing for the government to step in when parents are preventing children from receiving life-saving care. It's another when the government steps in to prevent parents from *pursuing* potentially life-saving care. And yet that's just what has happened repeatedly in the United Kingdom.

Why? Why would British society place parents' wishes below the wishes of the state? Because a bureaucratic society of experts generally sees parents as an obstacle to proper development. Parents, in this view, treat their children as chattel to be owned and trained—but the state can treat children with the dignity they are due. This means placing parental wishes to the side in every case in which those wishes come into conflict with the priorities of the state.

The bureaucrats of Britain don't merely usurp parental rights in the realm of life and death; they do so in the realm of upbringing as well. They have threatened religious Jewish schools for failing to inculcate children with LGBT propaganda; meanwhile, they have ignored the targeting of young women in Rotherham, Rochdale, Oxford and Newcastle because the perpetrators are disproportionately Muslim.

All of this is untenable, both morally and practically. Parents will not continue to give the power to control their children away to bureaucrats who do not know their children's names.

The Day the Iran Deal Died

May 9, 2018

Team Obama lives in a world of fiction.

As President Trump announced to the world that he would finally put a stake through the heart of the Iran deal—the signal foreign policy "achievement" of the Obama administration—Obama's former staffers lamented, rending their sackcloth and smearing their ashes. "I will never forget the dark cloud that hung over the White House in the years Iran was advancing nuclear program & Obama was briefed on all the risks of using military force," former United Nations Ambassador Samantha Power tweeted. "Trump has demolished America's credibility & paved the way for Iran to re-start its nuclear program. Trump has done the unthinkable: isolated the US & rallied the world around Iran."

Then there was amateur-fiction-writer-turned-professional-fiction-writer Ben Rhodes, a former Obama national security aide, who tweeted, "One tragicomic element of Trump's presidency is that the more he tries to tear down Obama's legacy, the bigger he makes Obama look." Meanwhile, former Secretary of State John Kerry, who had been traveling the world in an attempt to conduct his own personal foreign policy on behalf of the mullahs, stated, "Today's announcement weakens our security, breaks America's word, isolates us from our European allies, puts Israel at greater risk, empowers Iran's hardliners, and reduces our global leverage to address Tehran's misbehavior."

Obama himself stated, "Walking away from the JCPOA turns our back on America's closest allies."

In hearing all of these honeyed voices speak, one might think that Iran has been acting responsibly for the last three years, that it hasn't been pursuing a campaign of horrific terrorism in Yemen and Syria, that it hasn't been sponsoring the takeover of Lebanon by the terrorist group Hezbollah, that it hasn't been funding the Palestinian terror group Hamas, that it hasn't been developing long-range ballistic missiles while leading chants saying "Death to America." One might think that Obama left the Middle East a bright a beautiful place, not a hellhole filled with human carnage bought with dollars spent by Iran but funneled through the United States.

None of that is true, of course. Obama left the Middle East a smoking wreckage heap—a situation so grim that even Saudi Arabia, Egypt and Jordan have been forced to ally with Israel to allay fears of an Iranian regional takeover. Obama and his staff lied repeatedly to the American people about the Iran deal—and they continue to lie. When Kerry says that the deal will "empower Iran's hardliners," he is repeating an outright fabrication: The hardliners are in charge of the government, and the deal strengthened them. When Power speaks as though Obama alleviated the possibility of Iran's nuclear program, she's lying, too: The deal explicitly paved the way for an Iranian nuclear program free and clear of consequences from the international order. When Obama speaks as though our Middle East allies were pleased by the deal, he's lying: They all opposed it, and they're all celebrating its end.

Barack Obama had a peculiar vision of the Middle East remade: Iran ascendant, the power of Israel checked, the Saudis chastened. He achieved that vision at the cost of tens of thousands of lives across the region. President Trump is undoing that legacy. Good riddance.

Why Jerusalem Matters

May 16, 2018

This week, the Trump administration inaugurated the new American embassy in Jerusalem. The celebration in Israel was palpable; the embassy move came amidst the national celebration of the 70th anniversary of the creation of the state. The streets filled with Jews of all sorts, cheering and dancing.

Meanwhile, on the Gaza border, Hamas broadened its monthlong campaign to break down the Israel border, staging border "protests" attended by thousands—including terrorists who have used the supposed protests as a staging point for violent attacks on Israeli troops and territory. Palestinian terrorists have caused mass chaos, throwing Molotov cocktails at troops, attempting to rush the border, flinging explosives and tying incendiaries to kites in an attempt to set Israeli territory alight. The Israeli Defense Forces have responded with restraint. Despite this, a few dozen Palestinians have been killed, not the hundreds or thousands Hamas would presumably prefer.

But even as Yahya Sinwar, leader of Hamas in Gaza, suggested that "more than 100,000 people could storm the fence" between Israel and Gaza, and as 23-year-old Mohammed Mansoura announced, "We are excited to storm and get inside ... to kill, throw stones," the media covered the slow-rolling terror assault as a form of peaceful protest. A New York Times headline read "Israeli Troops Kill Dozens of Palestinian Protesters." A Wall Street Journal headline reads "Scores Killed, Thousands Injured as Palestinians Protest US Embassy Opening In Jerusalem."

Never mind that the riots had been going on for weeks preceding the embassy opening. Never mind that Hamas and the Palestinian Authority could quickly and permanently end all violence simply by stopping the violence. The real issue, according to the press, is President Trump and his Israeli friends.

What drives the leftist press's coverage? Simply put, antipathy to the West. Israel is seen as an outpost of colonialism by leftists, and has been since the 1967 war. Then-President Barack Obama expressed the view well in his 2009 speech in Cairo, suggesting that Israel's rationale relied on its "tragic history" that "culminated in an unprecedented Holocaust." In this view, the Palestinians were shunted aside in favor of providing national reparations to Jews; the Jews took their Western ways into the heart of a foreign region.

This isn't true. The living proof of that is Israel's eternal connection to Jerusalem. That's why both radical Muslims (including the Palestinian leadership) and the far left deny Israel's historic bond with its homeland and hope desperately to stop public recognition of that bond. If Israel exists because Jewish connection pre-existed everything else, then Israel isn't a new outpost of the West; it's the oldest center of the West. That's why Trump's announcement is important: It's a recognition that the West was founded on Jerusalem, rather than the other way around.

Peace will come when everyone recognizes what Trump has recognized: The Jewish connection to Jerusalem is unbreakable. And peace will come when Israel's enemies realize that violence can't change that underlying fact.

The Suicide of Europe

May 30, 2018

On Friday, the British police arrested Tommy Robinson, founder and former leader of the English Defence League, a far-right anti-Islam group. Robinson is a controversial character, to be sure, a sort of Milo Yiannopoulos lite. His chief focus is on the threat of radical Islam, which he believes threatens the integrity of the British system.

You don't have to like Robinson. But whatever you think of him, his arrest is absurd by any measure. You see, Robinson was arrested for standing outside a court building and reporting on a trial involving the alleged grooming of young girls for sexual assault by radical Muslims.

Now, what would be illegal about that, you ask? It turns out that Robinson was given a suspended sentence last year for filming outside another court building, where a trial for alleged gang rape by radical Muslims was taking place. He wasn't inside the courtroom. Nonetheless, the judge believed he was somehow biasing the jurors. According to the judge, Robinson was sentenced thanks to "pejorative language which prejudges the case, and it is language and reporting...that could have had the effect of substantially derailing the trial."

This time, Robinson was again arrested for prejudicing a case, only he wasn't inside the court building. He was outside. And the media were originally banned from reporting on his arrest so that *his* trial wouldn't be biased. In other words, Britain has now effectively banned reporting that actually mentions the Islamic nature of criminal defendants for fear of stirring up bigotry—and has banned reporting on reporting on such defendants. It's an infinite regress of suicidal political correctness.

But at least the Europeans have their priorities straight: While it's perfectly legal to lock up a provocateur covering a trial involving

Muslims, the European Union is now considering a ban on products like cotton buds, straws and other plastics for fear of marine litter. And just as importantly, it's now perfectly legal to kill unborn children again in Ireland, where voters—with the help of a cheering press—decided to lift the ban on abortions until the 20th week, condemning thousands of children to death.

This is how the West dies: with a tut-tut, not with a bang. The same civilization that sees it as a fundamental right to kill a child in the womb thinks it is utterly out of bounds to film outside a trial involving the abuse of children, so long as the defendants are radical Muslims. The Europeans have elevated the right to not be offended above the right to life; they've elevated the right to not be offended above the right to free speech, all in the name of some utopian vision of a society without standards.

Discarding those standards was supposed to make Europeans more free; it was supposed to allow Europeans to feel more comfortable. But the sad truth is that *no* society exists without certain standards and Europe has a new standard: enforcement of its "tolerance" via jail sentence, combined with tolerance of multiculturalism that sees tolerance itself as a Trojan horse. The notion of individual rights sprang from European soil. Now they're beginning to die there.

Nationalism and Patriotism
Don't Have to Be Opposites

November 14, 2018

On Sunday, French President Emmanuel Macron spoke at a ceremony marking the 100th anniversary of the end of World War I. There, he took the opportunity to slam President Trump's "America First" nationalism. "Patriotism," Macron said, "is the exact opposite of nationalism: Nationalism is a betrayal of patriotism. By putting our interests first, with no regard for others, we erase the very thing that a nation holds dearest, and the thing that keeps it alive: its moral values."

This statement has a sort of European charm. It's also false. And dangerous.

Nationalism, when opposed to patriotism, can indeed be terrible. It can suggest that the interests of one nation override the interests of every other nation, that imperialism and colonialism are worth pursuing out of love of blood and soil. But when combined with patriotism, nationalism can also be a bulwark against tyranny. Nationalism can stand up to international communism. Nationalism can refuse to bow before the dictates of multiculturalism, which suggest that all cultures and practices are of equal value.

Patriotism is a philosophy of national values: It is a statement that your nation has values that are eternal, true and noble. American patriotism prizes God-given individual rights protected by limited government. Were America to lose God-given individual rights protected by limited government, it would no longer be America. But patriotism doesn't mean that it is the job of America to spread our values everywhere else to the detriment of our own national strength. Our patriotism encompasses American nationalism: We believe that America must come first so that America can be strong enough to promote her values where appropriate.

It is simply a fact that human beings resonate to nationalism. The question is whether that nationalism can be grafted to a worthwhile philosophy. The German troops of World War I marched into battle out of national pride; so, too, did the American doughboys. Americans have fought and died for their flag and their families; so have soldiers of other nations. But America is great because that flag stands for certain values, and American families are built on those values.

The opposite of nationalism, then, isn't patriotism. It's internationalism, or the idea that all human beings share similar values, and that, therefore, borders and national interests are irrelevant. That philosophy is utterly foolish and dangerous. Simply view tape of thousands of radical Muslims marching in Pakistan to protest the acquittal of a Christian woman from charges of blasphemy and realize that not all people believe the same things.

But that multicultural philosophy has led Europe to open her borders to waves of migrants who may not share European values, and who have led to cultural polarization and, indeed, the rise of right-wing nationalist movements. It's that philosophy that has led Europe to leave behind her uniquely Western heritage in favor of a broader outlook that has undermined her cultural solidarity.

Nationalism, then, isn't the problem. Lack of values is. And mistaking anti-nationalism for a value system in and of itself endangers free citizens who hold worthwhile national values dear.

The 'International Community' Isn't a Community

December 12, 2018

Very often these days, we hear about the wonderful richness of the international community. Americans are chastised for failing to go along with the international community on climate change; failing to follow the consensus of the international community on health care; failing to mirror the priorities of the international community in foreign policy.

But here's the reality: There is no international community. There is merely a group of states motivated by self-interest. Sometimes those self-interests overlap. Other times they don't. But let's not pretend that the international community somehow maintains a sort of collective moral standing merely by dint of numbers. In fact, precisely the opposite is often true.

Take, for example, the United Nations' recent decision not to condemn the Palestinian terrorist group Hamas. This week, the U.N. General Assembly voted on a resolution condemning the group for "repeatedly firing rockets into Israel and for inciting violence, thereby putting civilians at risk," as well as for using assets to construct "tunnels to infiltrate Israel and equipment to launch rockets into civilian areas." The U.N., which requires a two-thirds vote to pass a General Assembly resolution, voted down the resolution—87 nations in favor, 58 against, 32 abstaining. All in all, that means that more nations voted against ratifying the resolution—90—than in favor of it.

Up to this point, the U.N. has never passed a single resolution against Hamas.

Just days later, Palestinian terrorists opened fire on a group of people waiting for a bus near Ofra, a settlement in Judea and Samaria. The drive-by shooting wounded seven people, including a pregnant woman and her unborn child, as well as her husband. Both the woman and the baby are now in critical condition; it will be a miracle if both survive. According to The Times of Israel, Hamas immediately praised the attack, deeming it "heroic" and an "affirmation of our people's choice and legitimacy in resisting the Zionist occupation and its settlers."

Hamas isn't hiding the ball. It is evil. It celebrates evil. It pays terrorists to commit acts of evil. But the international community isn't hiding the ball either when its members refuse to condemn terrorism as terrorism when it is directed against disfavored members of the international community.

Take, by contrast, the international community's reaction to a terrorist attack directed against an Iranian military parade in late September. The U.N. Security Council forcibly condemned the attack, calling it a "heinous and cowardly terrorist attack" and pledging its support to "hold perpetrators, organizers, financiers and sponsors of these reprehensible acts of terrorism accountable and bring them to justice."

What's the difference? Only the perpetrators and the targets. The international community is a joke. Perhaps the United States ought to change its climate change or health care or gun policies. But those arguments should never be made on the basis of the international standard of morality—a standard that doesn't exist, has never existed and ought not be the subject of pretending by Western nations that ought to know better.

Venezuela and the Myth of Kinder, Gentler Socialism

February 27, 2019

Venezuela is a socialist country. Venezuela is also a dictatorship. Currently, Venezuela has fallen into open violence and complete chaos, with the strongman Nicolas Maduro ordering troops to open fire on those attempting to bring humanitarian aid into the country.

Yet, strangely, Maduro still has his defenders. Sen. Bernie Sanders, I-Vt., the leading declared Democratic 2020 presidential candidate and avowed socialist, refuses to label Maduro a "dictator." Sen. Chris Murphy, D-Conn., said in full 9/11 truther mode, "Democrats need to be careful about a potential trap being set by Trump et al in Venezuela. Cheering humanitarian convoys sounds like the right thing to do, but what if it's not about the aid?" Fresh Face of the Democratic Party Rep. Alexandria Ocasio-Cortez, D-N.Y., has remained shockingly silent about Venezuela, except to tell The Daily Caller News Foundation, "I think that, you know, the humanitarian crisis is extremely concerning but, you know, when we use non-Democratic means to determine leadership, that's also concerning, as well." Rep. Ilhan Omar, D-Minn., another Fresh Face of the Democratic Party, grilled U.S. envoy to Venezuela Elliott Abrams in an obvious attempt to stall on behalf of a gentler approach to Maduro.

Why the shocking unwillingness by the socialist hard-liners in the Democratic Party to condemn Maduro and join the rest of the world in calling for his ouster? After all, we've been assured by Sanders, AOC, Omar and others that *true* socialism isn't at stake in Venezuela—*true* socialism can be found in nations like Sweden, Norway and Denmark. Yet even so, these socialist Democrats can't find it in their hearts to cut ties with Venezuela.

How strange.

Perhaps it's because Sanders and his crowd understand full well that Venezuela is an excellent case study in socialism—nationalization of major industries by a centralized government, abolition of the profit motive and redistribution of resources via tyranny. After all, it wasn't that long ago that Sanders was praising the Soviet Union (he said it had "a whole variety of programs for young people and cultural programs which go far beyond what we do in this country"), Nicaraguan Sandanista Daniel Ortega and Cuba's Fidel Castro ("... he educated their kids, gave their kids health care, totally transformed the society.").

And then there's the inconvenient fact that the countries that Sanders himself calls socialist totally reject the label. Former Swedish Prime Minister Carl Bildt launched into Sanders this week, stating, "Bernie Sanders was lucky to be able to get to the Soviet Union in 1988 and praise all its stunning socialist achievements before the entire system and empire collapsed under the weight of its own spectacular failures." In 2015, Danish Prime Minister Lars Rasmussen scoffed at Sanders' dreams of a socialist utopia, noting, "The Nordic model is an expanded welfare state which provides a high level of security to its citizens, but it is also a successful market economy with much freedom to pursue your dreams and life your life as you wish."

Here is the sad truth about socialism: Socialism drives economies into the ground in exact proportion to its prominence in the economy. Capitalism creates prosperity. It's convenient for Sanders and company to point to the Nordic countries as models of socialism when they are obviously founded on free markets, with socialistic redistribution schemes stacked atop that free market foundation. But deep down, Sanders knows that the truer reflection of socialism lies in Venezuela, Cuba and the Soviet Union. And that's why Sanders simply can't bring himself to disown Venezuelan socialism, even to prop up the lie that socialism wasn't truly tried in Venezuela.

How to Silence Debate, New Zealand Edition

March 20, 2019

Rep. Ilhan Omar, D-Minn., has unleashed a barrage of openly anti-Semitic commentary. She suggested that Israel had "hypnotized the world." She recently suggested that Jewish money lay behind American support for Israel. Finally, she suggested that American Israel supporters are representatives of dual loyalty. Her fellow Democrats shielded her from blowback by subsuming a resolution that condemns her anti-Semitism within a broader resolution that condemns intolerance of all types. Many of them suggested that labeling Omar's anti-Semitism actually represents a type of censorship—an attempt to quash debate about Israel, though none of Omar's comments even critiqued the Israeli government, and though many on the left have made anti-Israel arguments without invoking anti-Semitism.

Now Omar's defenders have come out of the woodwork to suggest that criticism of her anti-Semitism was somehow responsible for the white supremacist shooting of 50 innocent people in a mosque in Christchurch, New Zealand. Two protesters, New York University students and best friends Leen Dweik and Rose Asaf, confronted Chelsea Clinton, who had gently chided Omar for her Jew hatred. "After all that you have done, all the Islamophobia that you have stoked," Dweik screamed, "this, right here, is the result of a massacre stoked by people like you and the words you put out in the world. ... Forty-nine people died because of the rhetoric you put out there." Dweik, it should be noted, has called for the complete elimination of Israel.

Her message was parroted by terror supporter Linda Sarsour, who tweeted: "I am triggered by those who piled on Representative Ilhan Omar and incited a hate mob against her until she got assassination threats now giving condolences to our community.

What we need you to do is reflect on how you contribute to islamophobia and stop doing that."

Meanwhile, mainstream commentators attempted to use the New Zealand anti-Muslim terror attack to blame critics of radical Islam. Omer Aziz, writing for The New York Times, slammed Jordan Peterson for calling Islamophobia "a word created by fascists" and Sam Harris for calling it "intellectual blood libel." Bill Maher has come in for similar criticism; so have I, mostly for a video I cut in 2014 in which I read off poll statistics from various Muslim countries on a variety of topics, concluding that a huge percentage of Muslims believed radical things.

Here's the truth: Radical Islam is dangerous. The Islamic world has a serious problem with radical Islam. And large swaths of the Muslim world are, in fact, hostile to Western views on matters ranging from freedom of speech to women's rights. To conflate that obvious truth with the desire to murder innocents in Christchurch is intellectual dishonesty of the highest sort. If we want more Muslims living in liberty and freedom, we must certainly demolish white supremacism—and we must also demolish radical Islam, devotees of which were responsible for an estimated 84,000 deaths in 2017 alone, most of those victims Muslim.

And here's another truth: Anti-Semitism is ugly, whether it's coming from white supremacists or Ilhan Omar. Making that point has nothing to do with the killing of Muslims in Christchurch.

So long as the media continue to push the narrative that criticism of Islam is tantamount to incitement of murder, radical Islam will continue to flourish. So long as the media continue to cover for the dishonest argument that criticism of anti-Semitism forwards the goals of white supremacists, anti-Semitism will continue to flourish. Honest discussion about hard issues isn't incitement.

What We Can Learn From the European Union

May 29, 2019

The European Union Parliament elections this week provided a shock to the system for the center-right and center-left coalition in European politics: The big winners were nationalist movements. In France, Marine Le Pen's immigration-restrictionist National Front defeated the party of the current president, Emmanuel Macron. In Italy, Matteo Salvini's similarly anti-immigration League Party won big. Nationalist parties made gains in Poland, Hungary, Sweden and Great Britain. Euroscepticism is on the rise. And it is being met with a similarly fervent movement of the left: Greens and liberals did shockingly well in Germany.

The main driver behind the new polarization: increased power aggregated in Brussels. While the European Union parliament majority remains pro-EU and pro-immigration, polarization has broken out specifically as a result of the EU overstepping its original boundaries. As Daniel Hannan, Conservative MP and Brexit advocate, writes, "The EU, in short, is responding to the euro and migration crises in the way it responds to everything: with deeper integration."

The burgeoning conflict within the EU should provide the United States with an object lesson: When you maximize the power of the federal government at the expense of the states, you maximize the possibility of polarization. And indeed, that's precisely what we've seen.

Take, for example, transgender bathrooms. If ever there were a local issue, that would be one: What business is it of a New Yorker what North Carolinians do to their bathrooms? Yet North Carolina's bathroom laws prompted national boycotts from residents of other states. That's because the leftist mindset in the United States holds that the federal government ought to weigh in on every issue—and in the absence of federal intervention, informal boycotts should be utilized. Or how about abortion? The Constitution has a process for amendment—but barring such amendment, the issue of abortion remains state-defined in nature. Nonetheless, Netflix announced this week that it will consider boycotting Georgia if Georgia's "heartbeat bill" goes into effect; Sen. Cory Booker, D-N.J., among others, has stated that he wants federal legislation to encode Roe v. Wade.

It's not difficult to imagine these mutual recriminations spiraling. As leftists, motivated by the supposed best of intentions, dictate that the federal government radically escalate its intervention into state domains, conservatives will fight back. The founders recognized that a federal government that usurps state powers would result in the breakdown of the system itself. We're beginning to see that prophecy play out in Europe; the possibility of a similar progression in the United States seems more and more likely.

A system of defined powers is the only system likely to preserve the health and happiness of a diverse society. Whether the European Union survives will depend largely on whether the EU takes account of the inherent powers of the countries it represents; whether the United States survives in the long run will depend on whether the federal government continues to encroach on the power of localities and states without regard for the strictures of the Constitution.

In the Spotlight

It is your duty to examine the conduct of public figures and put them in the spotlight — that is your duty.
—Nelson Mandela

On Human Nature and Mike Pence's Dinner Partners

April 5, 2017

This week, the Washington Post published a long form piece about Vice President Mike Pence, which included a little tidbit that said, "In 2002, Mike Pence told the Hill that he never eats alone with a woman other than his wife and that he won't attend events featuring alcohol without her by his side, either." The left—and some elements of the secular-minded right—lost its ever-loving mind. Bret Stephens of the Wall Street Journal said this "religious fundamentalism" springs from "terror of women." Joanna Grossman of Vox called Pence's rule "probably illegal," saying it is "deeply damaging to women's employment opportunities."

Never mind that there's no evidence whatsoever of employment discrimination by Pence against women. Never mind that Pence's 30-plus year marriage is good evidence that his standards have worked for him and his wife in preserving their marriage. Pence is bad, and his standards are bad. What's more, they're theocratic insanity that wouldn't be out of place in countries ruled by Shariah.

What absolute horse pucky.

Pence isn't saying that every dinner with a woman potentially ends in the boudoir. He's saying that human beings are fallible, that they become particularly fallible away from their spouses in the wee hours, and that they become even more fallible than that around alcohol.

But this is one of the great foolish myths propagated by the left and now humored by even some on the right: that risk assessment by individual human beings, examining their own hearts, amounts to discrimination; that those who want to guard themselves from situations in which they are more likely to sin are somehow propagating societal myths.

It isn't true. Human beings sin. They sin because they are tempted. And they are tempted because they refuse to perform an honest assessment of their own hearts. Not all personal situations are created equal. A late-night dinner involving alcohol with a work colleague of the sex to which you could be attracted obviously carries more risk than working in the office with that same person in the middle of the day. Even leftists understand this, which is why there are significant restrictions on campus regarding male professors alone with female students and student-professor dating. As Damon Linker of The Week states: "What if morality requires social and cultural supports that limit individual freedom and that secular liberals are unwilling to forgo? ... Perhaps Pence's more morally traditional outlook has something in its favor—namely, realism."

Yet the left denies realism. It says that if Pence is tempted, that merely shows that his marriage is weak. The left's own logic with regard to sexual urges states that such urges are undeniable—so Pence must be perfect and asexual outside of marriage, or marriage itself is restrictive and nasty. To prove that his marriage is solid, therefore, Pence should be able to walk through a strip club without ever feeling a shred of temptation.

This is asinine. It's not how marriage works, and it's not how human beings work. It's not how life works, either. The left casts all individual sins at the feet of society, so it thinks that any prospective adultery must be the result of monogamy's evils or society's sexism. But no matter how you change social mores, people will sin and those they love will be hurt.

Unless, that is, people recognize their own limitations and set fences around themselves. That's not an act of discrimination or evil. That's an act of love—for a spouse, for a society and for a culture of decency that requires that we all take a long, hard look in the mirror before determining that we are incapable of sin.

Bill Clinton Won After All

November 29, 2017

Two weeks ago, it seemed that former President Bill Clinton was finished as a public figure. A variety of public intellectuals on the left had consigned him to the ashtray of history; they'd attested to their newfound faith in his rape accuser Juanita Broaddrick or torn him to shreds for having taken advantage of a young intern, Monica Lewinsky.

The moral goal was obvious: Set up a new intolerance for the sexual abuse of women. The political goal was even more obvious: Show that Democrats are morally superior to Republicans, and in doing so, shame Republicans into staying home rather than voting for Alabama Republican senatorial candidate Roy Moore, who has been credibly accused of sexual assault of minors.

Then it all fell apart.

On Sunday, House Minority Leader Nancy Pelosi, D-Calif.—the first female speaker of the House—brushed off Clinton's scandals with a simple one-liner: "Well, I think it's, obviously it is a generational change. But let me say the concern that we had then was that they were impeaching the president of the United States, and for something that had nothing to do with the performance of his duties."

Why would Pelosi defend Clinton? Because she also has to defend Sen. Al Franken, D-Minn., and Rep. John Conyers, D-Mich., both of whom have been accused of sexual harassment or sexual assault. And why would she have to defend either of them?

That's the $64,000 question. She really doesn't—just as the Democrats never had to defend Clinton. If they'd kept their mouths shut and let Clinton resign, then-Vice President Al Gore would have been president. There's a high likelihood he would have been re-elected in 2000. If the Democrats were to let Franken fall today, his replacement would be appointed by a Democratic governor of Minnesota. If they were to let Conyers go down, he'd be replaced in a special election in what The Cook Political Report deems a D+32 district, meaning it performed an average of 32 points more Democratic than the nation did as a whole in 2016. Democrats wouldn't miss a beat, and they'd have a shot at taking out Moore to boot. By defending Franken and Conyers, Democrats give Republicans ample opportunity to back Moore and point at Democratic hypocrisy all the while. While Republicans can at least point at the potential loss of a Senate seat to justify backing Moore, Democrats wouldn't suffer *any* loss by dumping Franken and Conyers.

There's only one real reason Pelosi would stand by accused Democrats: She doesn't care. Her logic with regard to Clinton is the only one that matters. He was a Democrat, and his sexual improprieties had nothing to do with his capacity for voting for her agenda. This was the national argument we had in 1998, and it was settled in Clinton's favor. Character doesn't matter. Only agenda does.

Republicans bucked that agenda. They don't anymore.

In order to shame Republicans, Democrats seemed to buck that agenda this time around. But that was all bluster.

Bill Clinton didn't just escape impeachment in 1998. He won the argument. He taught Americans that no matter how scummy our politicians might be, so long as they side with us on matters great or small, we ought to back them. We ought to back them not because our principles are important but because there might be some point in the future when our principles are at stake, and we don't want our feet held to the fire then, do we?

In the famous play "A Man for All Seasons," Sir Thomas More, betrayed by his former colleague Richard Rich in exchange for the post of attorney general in Wales, says: "Why, Richard, it profits a man nothing to give his soul for the whole world. ... But for Wales?" We're willing to give our souls for nothing. Or perhaps they're already gone.

The Grisly History of Chappaquiddick

April 4, 2018

On April 6, a bombshell will hit America's theaters.

That bombshell comes in the form of an understated, well-made, well-acted film called "Chappaquiddick." (Full disclosure: They advertise with my podcast.) The film tells the story of Ted Kennedy's 1969 killing of political aide Mary Jo Kopechne; the Massachusetts Democratic senator drove his car off a bridge and into the Poucha Pond, somehow escaped the overturned vehicle and left Kopechne to drown. She didn't drown, though. Instead, she reportedly suffocated while waiting for help inside an air bubble while Kennedy waited 10 hours to call for help. The Kennedy family and its associated political allies then worked to cover up the incident. In the end, Teddy was sentenced to a two-month suspended jail sentence for leaving the scene of an accident. The incident prevented Kennedy from running for president in 1972 and 1976, though he attempted a run in 1980 against then-President Jimmy Carter, failing.

So, why is the film important?

It's important because it doesn't traffic in rumors and innuendo—there is no attempt to claim that Kopechne was having an affair with Kennedy, or that she was pregnant with his child. It's important because it doesn't paint Kennedy as a monster but as a deeply flawed and somewhat pathetic scion of a dark and manipulative family. But most of all, it's important for two reasons: It's the first movie to actually tackle a serious Democratic scandal in the history of modern film, and it reminds us that Americans have long been willing to overlook scandal for the sake of political convenience.

First, there's the historic nature of the film. Here is an incomplete list of the films made about George W. Bush's administration since his election in 2000, nearly all of them accusatory in tone: "W," "Fahrenheit 9/11," "Recount," "Fair Game" and "Truth." There has still not been a movie made about former President Bill Clinton's impeachment (though one is apparently in the works). There's been no movie about former President Franklin Delano Roosevelt's internment of the Japanese, former President Lyndon Johnson's dramatic mishandling of the Vietnam War (though we have had two hagiographies of LBJ, one directed by Rob Reiner, the other starring Bryan Cranston) or former President Woodrow Wilson's racism and near fascism.

And it only took nearly 50 years to make a film about a Democratic icon leaving a woman to die in a river. It's amazing it was made in the first place.

Most importantly, though, "Chappaquiddick" reminds us that confirmation bias and wishful thinking aren't unique to one side of the aisle. In the era of President Trump, media members have had fun telling Republicans that they have abandoned all of their moral principles in order to back a man whose agenda they support. But Democrats beat Republicans there by decades: They not only overlooked a man who likely committed manslaughter but also made him into a hero, the "Lion of the Senate." We can't understand how morals and politics have been split in two without reckoning with this history.

"Chappaquiddick" is a must-see. It's just a shame it took half a century for it to see the light.

Oh, Say Kanye Sees

May 2, 2018

It's easy to dismiss Kanye West.

It's easy to dismiss him because he's nutty. This is a fellow who tweets about antique fish tanks and fur pillows. This is the guy who calls himself Yeezus (after Jesus) and suggested that then-President George W. Bush didn't care about black people in the aftermath of Hurricane Katrina. He isn't exactly known for his bouts of emotional stability.

And in our celebrity-driven culture, we shouldn't pay too much attention to those who haven't spent a lot of time studying policy. That's how we end up with celebrity politicians, emotion-driven policy and reality television substituting for news.

With that said, Kanye West did something deeply important over the last two weeks: He opened up the debate.

Stung by the gratuitous censorship of the left, West began tweeting that Americans ought to think for themselves. He even tweeted a picture of himself wearing a "Make America Great Again" hat. And suddenly, the left went nuts, too. Kumail Nanjiani, co-writer of "The Big Sick," tweeted, "This was the worst twitter day in twitter history." Op-eds ran at The Root and The Washington Post claiming that West had been suckered.

But surprisingly, West didn't back down. He soon released a track with fellow rapper T.I. debating the merits of coming out as pro-Trump, with T.I. tearing into him as out of touch and West defending himself as thinking outside "the plantation." West met with conservative activist Candace Owens and tweeted quotes from Thomas Sowell.

Now, none of this means that West should suddenly be considered for leadership of The Heritage Foundation. But it does mark a break in the solid leftist wall of Hollywood and the music industry, and in the intersectional coalition.

The entertainment industry can't tolerate conservatives—when I wrote a book on political bias in Hollywood, several Hollywood insiders told me openly that they refuse to hire those on the right. Shania Twain learned just a few weeks ago that signaling support for President Trump in any way means taking your career into your hands.

The same holds true in identity politics circles. Those on the left who suggest that politics must innately follow immutable biological characteristics (i.e. black people have to be Democrats) felt deeply threatened by West's comments. After Chance the Rapper tweeted out that black Americans don't have to vote Democrat, the left's pressure snapped into place so rigidly that he backed off and apologized.

But West hasn't.

What's happening? It's doubtful that West started reading Edmund Burke. It may just be that West, like a lot of Americans tired of being told what to think by their industry and racialists on all sides, is getting tired of being told what to do. It's possible that West, like most Americans, sees America as a place with problems but a place where individuals can think and achieve freely. And he's clearly willing to take part in a political debate so many of his friends aren't.

That makes West an important voice, at least for now. It does take courage to buck your entire cadre in order to publicly declare what you think. West deserves credit for that. And who knows? Perhaps some other prominent Americans might come forward to re-engage in a debate from which they have been barred.

The Banality of Bias

June 20, 2018

Peter Strzok is an FBI agent with a career spanning more than two decades. He was section chief of the counterespionage section in 2016 and thus in a position to oversee both the Hillary Clinton email investigation and the Russian election interference investigation. And he was supposedly perfect for the job: a Georgetown University graduate with a master's degree, married to a Securities and Exchange Commission official. Strzok was qualified and patriotic. He was a lifelong civil servant.

He was also a heavily biased, blatantly political bureaucrat.

Strzok, it turns out, was cheating on his wife with then-fellow FBI agent Lisa Page. Page and Strzok traded thousands of texts—so many that one is tempted to ask when they ever found time for their affair. The texts were extraordinarily political. Strzok hated President Trump and loved Clinton; his paramour felt the same. After the 2016 election, Strzok wrote, "Omg I am so depressed." Among those texts, a few stood out. First, one from Strzok to Page suggested that the Russia investigation could serve as an "insurance policy" against a Trump presidency. Second, in a text from Page to Strzok, she questions whether Trump would actually be president, and a response from Strzok reads, "We'll stop it." Third, a text from Strzok to Page after the election cycle and upon his involvement in the Robert Mueller probe reads, "For me, and this case, I personally have a sense of unfinished business."

All of these texts—and Strzok's conduct during the election cycle—led the Department of Justice inspector general to conclude that he couldn't exonerate Strzok from the charge of bias in his investigation. The IG report stated that Strzok's texts were "not only indicative of a biased state of mind but, even more seriously, implies a willingness to take official action to impact the presidential candidate's electoral prospects. This is antithetical to the core values of the FBI and the Department of Justice."

Here's the thing: Strzok wasn't alone. At least four other FBI agents sent pro-Clinton messages throughout the Clinton investigation. One agent stated that nobody would prosecute Hillary Clinton "even if we find unique classified" material on former Rep. Anthony Weiner's laptop. Another texted, "Vive le resistance" after the election. And the IG report subtly slip in this rather shocking revelation: "We identified numerous FBI employees, at all levels of the organization and with no official reason to be in contact with the media, who were nevertheless in frequent contact with reporters." That contact included employees receiving "benefits from reports," such as golf outings, drinks and meals.

This is how bureaucratic agencies lose legitimacy: not with overt acts of evil but through the echo-chamber mentality that exists in every social setting. We all live within cliques; we all deal with a select group of people. If that select group of people thinks alike, the group tends to radicalize over time. And if there are no checks in place—if that clique has enormous power—it's easy to see how cases can get botched.

This is the problem with unelected, unaccountable, nontransparent bureaucracies: They are subject to ideological perversion that they themselves may not even notice until it is too late. That's why they should be extraordinarily careful in how they wield power. Unfortunately, our law enforcement agencies aren't, and the result is a dramatic loss of trust that they can ill afford.

What Is Democratic Socialism?

July 18, 2018

The new rising star of the Democratic Party is Alexandria Ocasio-Cortez. The 28-year-old former bartender doesn't know much about politics—this week, she bungled her way through an interview answer by referring to Israeli "occupation" of Palestine and citing her lack of expertise on the issue despite her international relations degree. But she's young; she's energetic; and she speaks in glowing terms about rights to housing, food, college and health care. She's a charter member of the Democratic Socialists of America, a group, we're informed by The New York Times' Michelle Goldberg, that is on the rise. "Its growth has exploded since the 2016 election," Goldberg reports, "from 7,000 members to more than 37,000."

What exactly is democratic socialism, and what distinguishes it from socialism plain and simple? Ocasio-Cortez doesn't know. When asked about it by Meghan McCain on "The View," she stated that there is a "huge difference" between the two notions but then concluded, "I believe that in a moral and wealthy America, in a moral and modern America, no person should be too poor to live in this country." Which doesn't explain the difference at all.

The difference is truly between socialism and social democracy. Socialism suggests state ownership and control of all major resources—and generally ends with the complete collapse and destruction of the productive population. Social democracy suggests redistribution of capitalistic gains—more like Denmark or Norway or Sweden. It's unclear where Ocasio-Cortez lies on this spectrum considering that the DSA openly acknowledges its desire to abolish capitalism.

But let's assume that what Ocasio-Cortez and Democrats want is actually just European-style social democracy. If that's the case, they're still misreading the tea leaves: The Nordic countries aren't thriving and healthy because they're socialist; they're thriving and healthy because they are small and homogenous. In fact, Nordic lifestyles means that Nordic life expectancy outclassed life expectancy in the United States before the Nordic states tried to grow government redistributionism radically. The left is fond of citing Norway and Sweden—even though both are now moving in a politically right-wing direction—but neglecting Switzerland, which is just as successful and far less socialistic.

Furthermore, generous welfare policies can only operate in small, homogenous countries because if you open the borders to such countries, immigrants flood in and then sink the boat. That's why voters in Europe have been consistently moving toward a more restrictionist view of immigration—particularly in that bastion of social democracy, Sweden.

Yet the democratic socialist dream never dies, even as it fades away in Europe. Democrats will continue to point toward the Nordic states and claim that utopia is a mere "free lunch" program away. But lunch is never free, as a former bartender should know.

The Righteous Mission of Bernie Sanders

February 27, 2019

Sen. Bernie Sanders' perspective on the world is deeply wrong. He has spent his career defending oppressive socialist regimes across the planet while criticizing the supposed predation of the United States; he has generated no legislation of significance in decades of public service. His platform currently advocates for tax rates that mirror those of the Nordic countries, spending tens of trillions of dollars on various government-provided entitlements, and the destruction of well over 150 million people's private health insurance plans.

But there is one area in which Bernie Sanders represents the better angels of the Democratic nature: race.

Sanders is currently being excoriated by a radical segment of the Democratic Party for his racial views. Despite the fact that Sanders marched with Martin Luther King Jr. during the civil rights movement, he is now viewed as retrograde in his racial viewpoints. That's because he believes that socialism is a cure-all for racial discrimination. For example, Sanders refuses to endorse racial reparations, stating instead that broad-based governmental programs ought to benefit those who are lowest on the income ladder. He has likewise stated that candidates ought to be judged based on their ideas rather than their intersectional characteristics. In 2016, Sanders stated, "One of the struggles that you're going to be seeing in the Democratic Party is whether we go beyond identity politics."

Sanders, in other words, separates people by class rather than race. That's wrong, too: In America, we're all individuals who move between classes with remarkable rapidity. We are not the 1 percent and the 99 percent; in fact, a huge number of those in the top 1 percent every year were not in the 1 percent in prior years, and will not be again in future years. We do not have a stable hierarchy of income in the United States. Sanders, by his own statement, grew up in a lower-middle-class household in Brooklyn; he now has two vacation homes despite never having worked a serious job.

But if we're going to talk about damaging divisions in America, class divisions take a back seat to racial divisions. That's because America doesn't actually have a real history of class divisions—we've been an overwhelmingly middle-class country for centuries, as Alexis de Tocqueville noted. But our racial divisions have been all too real, marking the greatest blot on America's history.

Proponents of intersectional politics point this out, suggesting that those racial divisions continue to dominate American life. But that's simply not true. In reality, America is less racist now than it ever has been; laws that discriminate on the basis of race are unconstitutional; racial politics has been relegated, for the most part, to mind reading the supposed motives of political opponents. Sanders implicitly acknowledges that truth when he calls for solutions that do not take into account race as a key factor.

And for that sin, Sanders is being othered by many in the Democratic Party. He's viewed as old-fashioned, hopeful, naive—Trumplike in his view of race, a proponent of a hackneyed baby-boomer "Green Book" mentality. He's outdated and wrong.

Thus Sanders must be ousted for his failure to conform to the intersectional politics that now dominate the Democratic Party. But here's the thing: At least when it comes to his implicit treatment of race, Sanders is closer to the truth than his Democratic opponents. And if Democrats don't recognize this, they'll be abandoning the possibility of a broad-based coalition that crosses racial lines in favor of a racially polarized one that exacerbates them.

Criticism of Ilhan Omar Isn't Incitement

April 17, 2019

A couple of years ago, I spoke at the University of California, Berkeley. My presence was apparently so offensive to a particular group of people that hundreds of police officers were necessary to ensure the safety of the event. As I spoke inside, the protesters milled about, chanting and shouting. One of their favorite ditties: "SPEECH IS VIOLENCE!"

This, of course, is patent nonsense. Speech is not violence—and violence is not speech. Equating the two is the hallmark of a tyrannical worldview: If I can treat your speech as violence, then I am justified in using violence to suppress your speech. And yet that obvious fallacy has become the rallying cry in defense of execrable Rep. Ilhan Omar, D-Minn.

Omar, who has been content to spout openly anti-Semitic nonsense every several weeks since her election, came under fire this week for her remarks at an event in late March, shortly after her Democratic colleagues covered for her Jew hatred by watering down a resolution of condemnation. Speaking before the historically Hamas-friendly Council on American-Islamic Relations (CAIR), Omar unleashed a barrage of lies about the maltreatment of Muslims throughout America. In the midst of that barrage, she dropped a line about Sept. 11: "CAIR was founded after 9/11 because they recognized that some people did something and that all of us were starting to lose access to our civil liberties."

That minimization of 9/11—and that's what it is—resulted in blowback from conservatives. It's not as though Omar's history of treating terrorism with kid gloves is anything new, after all. In 2013, Omar did an interview in which she chided one of her professors for treating terrorist groups with horror while failing to do the same to America, England and the military: "The thing that was interesting in the class was every time the professor said 'Al Qaida,' his shoulders went up. ... But you know, it is that you don't say 'America' with an intensity. You don't say 'England' with the intensity. You don't say 'the Army' with the intensity."

In 2016, Omar wrote a letter to a judge asking for lighter sentences for men accused of being Islamic State group recruits, noting that these men merely "chose violence to combat direct marginalization" and calling their recruitment "a consequential mistake" that resulted from "systematic alienation."

In 2017, Omar wrote for Time magazine: "We must confront that our nation was founded by the genocide of indigenous people and on the backs of slaves, that we maintain global power with the tenor of neocolonialism. ... Our national avoidance tactic has been to shift the focus to potential international terrorism." That's not exactly a ringing rebuke of international terrorism.

But now Omar is criticizing those who merely quote her as inciting violence. She has claimed that President Trump, who posted a video that juxtaposed footage of 9/11 with her "some people did something" comment, is responsible for an uptick in the number of death threats she has received. Her close friend Rep. Alexandria Ocasio-Cortez, D-N.Y., went so far as to compare Omar to a victim of the Holocaust.

This is immoral in the extreme. Omar isn't a victim because she's being criticized. And speech isn't incitement. Sen. Bernie Sanders wasn't responsible for the congressional baseball game shooting. Former President Barack Obama wasn't responsible for the Dallas police shooting. And Trump isn't responsible for those who send Omar death threats. He's responsible for criticizing her—rightly, in this case. Democrats who hide behind the charge of incitement are simply attempting to quash debate. And that's far more dangerous for the future of America than criticizing a radical politician.

Can Joe Biden Apologize His Way
to the Presidency?

May 1, 2019

Former vice president and new 2020 Democratic frontrunner Joe Biden has a problem. His problem is simple: He has a record. That record is long and checkered. And that means that Biden has spent the first months of his undeclared campaign apologizing.

In January, Biden apologized for having supported criminal sentencing laws that helped drive down crime in the United States. He did so because those laws are now considered both passe and un-woke—they've been maligned as inherently racist. Thus, Biden stated: "I haven't always been right. I know we haven't always gotten things right, but I've always tried," adding that the bill in the early 1990s "trapped an entire generation" and "was a big mistake when it was made." That's a change from 2016, when Biden told CNBC he wasn't ashamed "at all" for supporting the bill and bragged, "I drafted the bill."

Weeks ago, as Biden prepped his presidential run, he approached Anita Hill, the woman who accused Justice Clarence Thomas of sexual harassment. Hill's testimony was riddled with inconsistencies and outright lies. Biden recognized that at the time—according to former Sen. Arlen Specter's autobiography, Biden told him in 1998 that, with regard to Hill's protestations of memory lapses, "It was clear to me from the way she was answering the questions, she was lying." Now, however, Biden told Hill, "I'm sorry for what happened to you." Hill, for her part, is having none of it—she called his apology insufficient and stated that he owes Americans a more generalized apology.

Then, just four weeks ago, Biden issued a quasi-apology for his habitual invasion of women's personal space. In a two-minute video, he explained: "The boundaries of protecting personal space have been reset. I get it. I get it. I hear what they're saying. I understand. And I'll be much more mindful."

All of this has prompted Damon Linker of The Week to forecast: "Biden will apologize. And then apologize again. And then again. Endlessly. Gracelessly. Until he finally gives up and goes home."

Amazingly, though, all of the things for which Biden is apologizing are things for which he *should not be apologizing*. The early 1990s saw a spike in crime that largely affected minority communities; Hill was probably prevaricating; Biden's invasion of personal space is awkward, but it was never harassment. But in our new political world, running means having to say you're sorry for having a record at all. That's why it was easier for Barack Obama to run than Hillary Clinton—and, in many ways, it was easier for Donald Trump to run than Sen. Ted Cruz. Having a record is a burden.

The power of positive thinking trumps years of experience. After all, you don't have to worry about what Mayor Pete Buttigieg has done since he's never done anything. But you *do* have to worry about Joe Biden's record being rehashed. That's why Biden's best weeks may be his first weeks. As his record reemerges, as other Democrats dig into his past for dirt, Biden will have to get used to saying he's sorry and then hope that Democratic voters choose to take him back.

The Dis-Grace of Harvard

June 19, 2019

This week, Parkland survivor Kyle Kashuv announced that Harvard University has withdrawn his acceptance to the college. In the aftermath of the mass shooting at Marjory Stoneman Douglas High School, the then-high school junior became a prominent voice for school safety, meeting with politicians across the political spectrum. He was also a prominent defender of Second Amendment rights. After scoring 1550 on his SATs and graduating second in his class, Kashuv was admitted to Harvard, turning down scholarship money at other schools to do so.

Then came the tsunami.

Former classmates who oppose Kashuv's politics revealed on social media that when he was 16, months before the Parkland shooting, he typed egregious racist slurs, including the N-word, in a private Google doc. This revelation led Kashuv to immediately apologize publicly for his use of the language, which he insisted was not a reflection of racist belief but a juvenile attempt to shock his peers. He pointed to his record of public-facing accomplishment and pledged to learn from his mistakes. He issued an apology to Harvard, taking full responsibility for his comments; he reached out to the Office of Diversity and Inclusion to see what steps he could take to assure them that he had changed.

No matter. Harvard's admissions committee decided to withdraw his acceptance.

There are several lessons here—all of them bad for the country.

First, grace is no longer an aspect of American life—at least for one side of the aisle. Kashuv has been in the public eye for a year and a half. In that time, he has acted with remarkable poise, as have many others in his class. The fact that he participated in an idiotic and disgusting private group chat months before the Parkland shooting has had apparently no effect on his public behavior. If the new standard is that past private statements, once surfaced, override all public behavior since—including apologies, evidence of decency and willingness to evidence repentance—we are entering a dangerous new era. Is Harvard prepared for dredging up every incoming first year's Twitter direct messages for scrutiny?

But that won't be the standard, obviously. The commentariat calling for Kashuv's expulsion was loudly decrying Harvard for having barred Michelle Jones, who *killed her own 4-year-old*, just two years ago. The problem for Kashuv is that he is conservative; the old racist slurs were merely a means of damaging him. There is little question that were pro-gun control David Hogg the Parkland survivor at issue rather than Kashuv, a little more grace might have been applied here.

Second, public life comes with inherent risks and thus should be avoided by rational actors. Kashuv would have been admitted to Harvard if he had never engaged in activism: He scored a 1550 on his SAT and graduated second in his class. No one on the radical left or alt-right would have tried to destroy his academic career; no one would have bothered. Kashuv dared to speak up politically and thus became a target. Rational actors will take note and stay away from the public square, leaving that square to the most shameless and the most enigmatic.

Third, Harvard has become an institution not for education but for capitulation to the mob. Forget Kashuv for a second. Focus instead on Harvard Law School professor Ronald Sullivan, a political liberal who was tossed as dean of a residential house for the grave sin of acting as a defense attorney on Harvey Weinstein's team. Cross Harvard's most radical students or the wokescolds on social media and the administration will capitulate in short order.

Kashuv will be fine. He'll move on, go to another school, mature and grow. But Harvard won't be a part of that process. The social media mob was motivated not by a desire to purify by our politics—after all, Ralph Northam is still governor of Virginia—but by a desire to damage the Parkland student they just didn't like.

About the Author

Ben Shapiro was born in 1984. He entered the University of California Los Angeles at the age of 16 and graduated summa cum laude and Phi Beta Kappa in June 2004 with a Bachelor of Arts degree in Political Science. He graduated Harvard Law School cum laude in June 2007.

Shapiro was hired by Creators Syndicate at age 17 to become the youngest nationally syndicated columnist in the United States. His columns are printed in major newspapers and websites including *The Riverside Press-Enterprise* and the *Conservative Chronicle*, Townhall.com, ABCNews.com, WorldNetDaily.com, Human Events, FrontPageMag.com, and FamilySecurityMatters.com. His columns have appeared in *The Christian Science Monitor, Chicago Sun-Times, Orlando Sentinel, The Honolulu Advertiser, The Arizona Republic, Claremont Review of Books,* and RealClearPolitics.com. He has been the subject of articles by *The Wall Street Journal, The New York Times*, The Associated Press, and *The Christian Science Monitor*. He has been quoted on "The Rush Limbaugh Show" and "The Dr. Laura Show," at CBSNews.com, and in the *New York Press, The Washington Times*, and *The American Conservative*.

Shapiro is the author of best-sellers *Brainwashed: How Universities Indoctrinate America's Youth, Porn Generation: How Social Liberalism Is Corrupting Our Future,* and *Project President: Bad Hair and Botox on the Road to the White House.* He has appeared on hundreds of television and radio shows around the nation, including *The O'Reilly Factor, Fox and Friends, In the Money, DaySide with Linda Vester, Scarborough Country, The Dennis Miller Show, Fox News Live, Glenn Beck Show, Your World with Neil Cavuto, 700 Club, The Laura Ingraham Show, The Michael Medved Show, The G. Gordon Liddy Show, The Rusty*

Humphries Show, "*The Lars Larson Show*, *The Larry Elder Show*, *The Hugh Hewitt Show*, and *The Dennis Prager Show*.

Shapiro is married and runs Benjamin Shapiro Legal Consulting in Los Angeles.

Facts Don't Care About Your Feelings
is also available as an e-book
for Kindle, Amazon Fire, iPad, Nook and
Android e-readers. Visit
creatorspublishing.com to learn more.

o o o

CREATORS PUBLISHING

We publish books.
We find compelling storytellers and
help them craft their narrative,
distributing their novels and collections
worldwide.

o o o